Japanese 1

Grammar and Vocabulary Workbook

Japanese Tutor
Grammar and Vocabulary Workbook

Shin-Ichiro Okajima

First published in Great Britain in 2015 by Hodder and Stoughton. An Hachette UK company.

This edition published in 2015 by John Murray Learning

British Library Cataloguing in Publication Data: a catalogue record for this title is available from the British Library.

Library of Congress Catalog Card Number: on file.

ISBN: 9781444799835

3

The publisher has used its best endeavours to ensure that any website addresses referred to in this book are correct and active at the time of going to press. However, the publisher and the author have no responsibility for the websites and can make no guarantee that a site will remain live or that the content will remain relevant, decent or appropriate.

The publisher has made every effort to mark as such all words which it believes to be trademarks. The publisher should also like to make it clear that the presence of a word in the book, whether marked or unmarked, in no way affects its legal status as a trademark.

Every reasonable effort has been made by the publisher to trace the copyright holders of material in this book. Any errors or omissions should be notified in writing to the publisher, who will endeavour to rectify the situation for any reprints and future editions.

Typeset by Cenveo® Publisher Services.

Printed and bound in Great Britain by CPI Group (UK) Ltd., Croydon, CR0 4YY.

John Murray Learning policy is to use papers that are natural, renewable and recyclable products and made from wood grown in sustainable forests. The logging and manufacturing processes are expected to conform to the environmental regulations of the country of origin.

Carmelite House
50 Victoria Embankment
London EC4Y 0DZ
www.hodder.co.uk

CONTENTS

MEET THE AUTHOR

Shin-Ichiro Okajima has lived and worked in UK for more than 20 years. He is currently a Language Specialist at SOAS Language Centre, where his duties include managing and updating all part time Japanese short courses, as well as convening the Certificate/Diploma in Communicative Japanese.

ACKNOWLEDGEMENTS

I would like to thank the following people for their invaluable comments, feedback and support in writing this workbook:

Steven James Martin, Frances Amrani, Robert Williams at Hodder and Stoughton, and a big thanks to Helga and Tamotsu for putting up with me while writing this book.

I would like to dedicate this book to my late father, Ginjiro Okajima.

SCOPE AND SEQUENCE OF UNITS

UNIT	CEFR	TOPIC	LEARNING OUTCOME
UNIT 1 Pages 2–11	A2	Personal information	Greetings Expressing personal information
UNIT 2 Pages 12–23	B1	Daily routines	Inviting others to do things Talking about daily routines and future Expressing how often actions take place
UNIT 3 Pages 24–35	B1	Shopping	Talking about location Talking about quantity
UNIT 4 Pages 36–47	B1	Leisure time	Talking about the past Talking about giving and receiving Telling the time Expressing desires
UNIT 5 Pages 48–57	B1	People and places	Describing people, places and objects Giving opinions
UNIT 6 Pages 58–67	B1	Transport and travel	Describing experiences Expressing opinion and hopes
UNIT 7 Pages 68–77	B1	Likes and dislikes	Expressing ability, desire and preferences Expressing wanting to do something Expressing two actions taking place simultaneously Expressing how to do something Expressing going somewhere to do things
UNIT 8 Pages 78–87	B1	Visiting a friend	Identifying the Japanese verb groups Describing sequences of actions Expressing requests Giving and understanding directions

LANGUAGE		SKILLS		
GRAMMAR	**VOCAB**	**READING**	**WRITING**	**KANJI**
Present tense Basic copular structure XはYです。 (の as possessive and copula) これVSこの	Greeting Introduction Profession Family Nationality Numbers 1–10	Dialogue introducing personal information	Parargraph about personal information	私、日、月、本、人
Masu form, present tense Particles Future plans	Time expressions Place names Food and drink Routine verbs Pronouns	Description about a daily routine	Description about a daily routine	火、水、木、金、土
Existence and counters Location words and word order Subject marker	Shopping Counters Numbers above 100 Everyday objects	Dialogue about shopping	Description of a room	男、女、子、円、中
Past tense Tai form	Months of the year Days of week Hobbies and leisure time	Blog	Diary entry for a whole day	何、時、分、食、飲
Adjective present tense Asking questions where to put "na" in sentences	Adjectives Degree adverbs	Email	Note describing family members	大、小、高、低、長
Adjective past tense Particle で	Adverbs from adjectives Weather Seasons Transport and travel	Blog	Report about a holiday experience	天、気、雨、電、車
Use of the particle が to mark grammatical objects Use of the masu form stem Superlative	Sports Music Hobby Food and drink Degree adverbs Occupation	Dialogue about likes and dislikes	Self-introduction on a social media site	上、下、手、好、語
て form て form plus **kudasai** Japanese verb groups	Daily routines Directions	Dialogues about routines	Description of a weekend	行、来、見、右、左

Permission and prohibition using て form.	Verbs that trigger the particle に	Blog	Report about the law and age restrictions	入、出、話、休
Progressive tense using て form plus **imasu** Particle で Present perfect using **mou** and **mada**	Time adverbs *now, yet* and *already*	Dialogue at a party	Self-Introduction	今、学、校、生
Use of て form Particle に	Clothing	Blog	An account about last Christmas	先、父、母、白
Plain form, present tense	Hobbies	Blog introducing a friend	Writing about a friend's interests and hobbies	聞、読、書、前
Plain form, present tense	Time expressions	Email	Email about holiday plans	国、外、友、名
Plain form, past tense	Frequency adverbs Holiday activities	Text about experiences	Writing about experiences which can be used at a party for social interaction	山、年、間、後
Plain form, past tense Comparatives Subordinate clause containing *when*	Spare time activities and advice	Biography	Autobiography	午、毎、川、海
Plain volitional form Particle が	Duration of time (months) Work House chores	Dialogue about New Year's resolutions	Description of New Year's resolutions	一、二、三、四

Plain negative form, present and past tense Plain forms of adjectives and nouns	Routine verbs	Blog about a busy day	Blog about a busy day	五、六、七、八
Plain forms Use of the particle が to mark grammatical subjects	Duration of time (weeks, years)	Email	Email about changing job and an invitation	九、十、百、千
Other uses of the plain negative form Particles revision	Work	Notes about a business trip	Diary plans for a business trip	万、半、曜、週
Conditional forms Plain form, past tense (affirmative and negative)	Education	A composition about future career plans	Plans for future career	口、東、西、南、北

HOW TO USE THIS BOOK

If you have studied Japanese before and have reached a beginner level but would like to improve your grammar, vocabulary, reading and writing skills, this is the book for you. *Japanese Tutor* is a grammar workbook which contains a comprehensive grammar syllabus from beginner to pre-intermediate and combines grammar and vocabulary presentations with over 200 practice exercises.

The language you will learn is presented through concise explanations, engaging exercises, simple infographics, and personal tutor tips. The infographics present complex grammar points in an accessible format while the personal tutor tips offer advice on correct usage, colloquial alternatives, exceptions to rules, etc. Each unit contains reading comprehension activities incorporating the grammar and vocabulary taught as well as a freer writing and real-life tasks. The reading stimuli include emails, blogs, social media posts and business letters using real language so you can be sure you're learning vocabulary and grammar that will be useful for you.

You can work through the workbook by itself or you can use it alongside our *Complete Japanese* course. This workbook has been written to reflect and expand upon the content of *Complete Japanese* and is a good place to go if you would like to practise your reading and writing skills on the same topics.

There are lots of philosophies and approaches to language learning, some practical, some quite unconventional, and far too many to list here. Perhaps you know of a few, or even have some techniques of your own. In this book we have incorporated the Discovery Method of learning, a sort of awareness-raising approach to language learning. This means that you will be encouraged throughout to engage your mind and figure out the language for yourself, through identifying patterns, understanding grammar concepts, noticing words that are similar to English, and more. This method promotes language awareness, a critical skill in acquiring a new language. As a result of your own efforts, you will be able to better retain what you have learnt, use it with confidence, and, even better, apply those same skills to continuing to learn the language (or, indeed, another one) on your own after you've finished this book.

Everyone can succeed in learning a language – the key is to know how to learn it. Learning is more than just reading or memorizing grammar and vocabulary. It's about being an active learner, learning in real contexts, and, most importantly, using what you've learned in different situations. Simply put, if you figure something out for yourself, you're more likely to understand it. And when you use what you've learnt, you're more likely to remember it.

As many of the essential but (let's admit it!) challenging details, such as grammar rules, are introduced through the Discovery Method, you'll have more fun while learning. Soon, the language will start to make sense and you'll be relying on your own intuition to construct original sentences independently, not just reading and copying.

Enjoy yourself!

BECOME A SUCCESSFUL LANGUAGE LEARNER

1   Make a habit out of learning

Study a little every day, between 20 and 30 minutes is ideal. Give yourself **short-term goals**, e.g. work out how long you'll spend on a particular unit and work within this time limit, and **create a study habit**. Try to **create an environment conducive to learning** which is calm and quiet and free from distractions. As you study, do not worry about your mistakes or the things you can't remember or understand. Languages settle gradually in the brain. Just **give yourself enough time** and you will succeed.

2   Maximize your exposure to the language

As well as using this book, you can listen to radio, watch television or read online articles and blogs. Do you have a personal passion or hobby? Does a news story interest you? Try to access Japanese information about them. It's entertaining and you'll become used to a range of writing and speaking styles.

3   Vocabulary

Group new words under **generic categories**, e.g. *food, furniture*, **situations** in which they occur, e.g. under *restaurant* you can write *waiter, table, menu, bill*, and **functions**, e.g. *greetings, parting, thanks, apologizing*.

▶   Write the words over and over again. Keep lists on your smartphone or tablet, but remember to switch the keyboard language so you can include all accents and special characters.
▶   Cover up the English side of the vocabulary list and see if you remember the meaning of the word. Do the same for the Japanese.
▶   Create flash cards, drawings and mind maps.
▶   Write Japanese words on post-it notes and stick them to objects around your house.
▶   **Experiment with words.** Look for patterns in words, e.g. [derive terms for nationalities by adding -**jin** to country names: **Furansu/Furansu-jin**]

4   Grammar

Experiment with grammar rules. Sit back and reflect on how the rules of Japanese compare with your own language or other languages you may already speak.

▶   Use known vocabulary to practise new grammar structures.
▶   When you learn a new verb form, write the conjugation of several different verbs you know that follow the same form.

5   Reading

The passages in this book include questions to help guide you in your understanding. But you can do more:

▶   **Imagine the situation.** Think about what is happening in the extract/passage and make educated guesses, e.g. a postcard is likely to be about things someone has been doing on holiday.
▶   **Guess the meaning of key words before you look them up.** When there are key words you don't understand, try to guess what they mean from the context.
▶   If you're reading a Japanese text and cannot get the gist of a whole passage because of one word or phrase, try to look at the words around that word and see if you can work out the meaning from context.

6 Writing

Practice makes perfect. The most successful language learners know how to overcome their inhibitions and keep going.

▶ When you write an email to a friend or colleague, or you post something on social media, pretend that you have to do it in Japanese.
▶ When completing writing exercises see how many different ways you can write it, imagine yourself in different situations and try answering as if you were someone else.
▶ Try writing longer passages such as articles, reviews or essays in Japanese, it will help you to formulate arguments and convey your opinion as well as helping you to think about how the language works.
▶ Try writing a diary in Japanese every day, this will give context to your learning and help you progress in areas which are relevant to you.

7 Visual learning

Have a look at the infographics in this book, do they help you to visualize a useful grammar point? You can keep a copy of those you find particularly useful to hand to help you in your studies, or put it on your wall until you remember it. You can also look up infographics on the Internet for topics you are finding particularly tricky to grasp, or even create your own.

8 Learn from your errors

▶ Making errors is part of any learning process, so don't be so worried about making mistakes that you won't write anything unless you are sure it is correct. This leads to a vicious circle: the less you write, the less practice you get and the more mistakes you make.
▶ Note the seriousness of errors. Many errors are not serious as they do not affect the meaning.

9 Learn to cope with uncertainty

▶ Don't over-use your dictionary.
  Resist the temptation to look up every word you don't know. Read the same passage several times, concentrating on trying to get the gist of it. If after the third time some words still prevent you from making sense of the passage, look them up in the dictionary.

JAPANESE WRITING

Japanese is written using a combination of three distinct scripts: *Hiragana, Katakana* and *Kanji* (Chinese characters). Hiragana and Katakana are phonetic scripts, meaning that each character represents a sound. Katakana is used for foreign names, places and objects. There are 46 basic letters for both Hiragana and Katakana, plus about 55 modified letters. Together they make up the 101 basic sounds of Japanese. Kanji, on the other hand, are ideographs, conveying meaning as well as sounds.

私はイギリス人です。

Watashi wa Igirisu-jin desu.

I am British.

Kanji: 私, 人
Hiragana: は, です
Katakana: イギリス

Roman alphabets and Arabic numerals are also used in Japanese writing.

CDを2まい買いました。

CD o ni-mai kaimashita.

I bought two CDs.

Kanji: 買
Hiragana: を, まい, いました
Roman alphabet: CD
Numerals: 2

Japanese sounds are made of *mora*, which is a unit of sound. A mora can be represented by Hiragana and Katakana. A mora consists of either vowels or a combination of consonants and vowels, e.g. **a**, **wa**, **ta**, **shi**, etc., except the 'n' sound, which can be a mora by itself. They are pronounced with equal length when spoken. In the following table, Hiragana are written on the left while Katakana are written in brackets.

Basic mora

VOWELS	A	I	U	E	O
	a あ (ア)	i い (イ)	u う (ウ)	e え (エ)	o お (オ)
k-	ka か (カ)	ki き (キ)	ku く (ク)	ke け (ケ)	ko こ (コ)
s-	sa さ (サ)	shi し (シ)	su す (ス)	se せ (セ)	so そ (ソ)
t-	ta た (タ)	chi ち (チ)	tsu つ (ツ)	te て (テ)	to と (ト)
n-	na な (ナ)	ni に (ニ)	nu ぬ (ヌ)	ne ね (ネ)	no の (ノ)
h-	ha は (ハ)	hi ひ (ヒ)	fu ふ (フ)	he へ (ヘ)	ho ほ (ホ)
m-	ma ま (マ)	mi み (ミ)	mu む (ム)	me め (メ)	mo も (モ)
y-	ya や (ヤ)		yu ゆ (ユ)		yo よ (ヨ)
r-	ra ら (ラ)	ri り (リ)	ru る (ル)	re れ (レ)	ro ろ (ロ)
w-	wa わ (ワ)				wo を (ヲ)
n	n ん (ン)				

Modified mora I

g	ga が (ガ)	gi ぎ (ギ)	gu ぐ (グ)	ge げ (ゲ)	go ご (ゴ)
z	za ざ (ザ)	ji じ (ジ)	zu ず (ズ)	ze ぜ (ゼ)	zo ぞ (ゾ)
d	da だ (ダ)	ji ぢ (ヂ)	zu づ (ヅ)	de で (デ)	do ど (ド)
b	ba ば (バ)	bi び (ビ)	bu ぶ (ブ)	be べ (ベ)	bo ぼ (ボ)
p	pa ぱ (パ)	pi ぴ (ピ)	pu ぷ (プ)	pe ぺ (ペ)	po ぽ (ポ)

Modified mora II
(consonants plus small ya, yu, yo)

kya きゃ (キャ)	kyu きゅ (キュ)	kyo きょ (キョ)
sha しゃ (シャ)	shu しゅ (シュ)	sho しょ (ショ)
cha ちゃ (チャ)	chu ちゅ (チュ)	cho ちょ (チョ)
nya にゃ (ニャ)	nyu にゅ (ニュ)	nyo にょ (ニョ)
hya ひゃ (ヒャ)	hyu ひゅ (ヒュ)	hyo ひょ (ヒョ)

mya	みゃ	(ミャ)	myu	みゅ	(ミュ)	myo	みょ	(ミョ)
rya	りゃ	(リャ)	ryu	りゅ	(リュ)	ryo	りょ	(リョ)
gya	ぎゃ	(ギャ)	gyu	ぎゅ	(ギュ)	gyo	ぎょ	(ギョ)
ja	じゃ	(ジャ)	ju	じゅ	(ジュ)	jo	じょ	(ジョ)
bya	びゃ	(ビャ)	byu	びゅ	(ビュ)	byo	びょ	(ビョ)
pya	ぴゃ	(ピャ)	pyu	ぴゅ	(ピュ)	pyo	ぴょ	(ピョ)

Double consonants

kk, pp, ss, tt, etc.	silent mora つ (ッ)

Long vowels

ā, aa	ああ	(アー)
ī, ii	いい	(イー)
ū, uu	うう	(ウー)
ē, ei, ee	ええ、えい	(エー)
ō, ou, oo	おう、おお	(オー)

Examples

KiNeN (ki-n-e-n) きんえん *no smoking*

KineN (ki-ne-n) きねん *anniversary, memory*

byouiN (byo-u-i-n) びょういん *hospital*

biyouiN (bi-yo-u-i-n) びよういん *beautician*

kata (ka-ta) かた *shoulder*

katta (ka-t-ta) かった *bought*

koko (ko-ko) ここ *here*

kōkō (ko-u-ko-u) こうこう *high school*

Special Katakana mora
(consonants and vowels plus small vowels)

The following Katakana letters represent sounds that are not original Japanese sounds. They are used to represent foreign loanwords.

		wi	ウィ			we	ウェ	wo	ウォ
va	ヴァ	vi	ヴィ			ve	ヴェ	vo	ヴォ
						she	シェ		
						je	ジェ		
						che	チェ		
tsa	ツァ					tse	ツェ	tso	ツォ
		ti	ティ	tu	トゥ				
		di	ディ	du	ドゥ (デュ)				
fa	ファ	fi	フィ			fe	フェ	fo	フォ

Kanji

Jōyō Kanji is the standardized list of 2,136 common Kanji, announced officially by the Japanese Ministry of Education (published in 2010). It is intended as a baseline for compulsory education and use in official documents. In this workbook, 89 frequently-used Kanji are introduced for recognition.

Many Kanji have several pronunciations or 'readings'. This is because Japanese uses a lot of Chinese-style words as well as Japanese words. You therefore need to know the context in which a Kanji is used to determine its pronunciation. The Japanese style reading is called **kun yomi**, while the Chinese style reading is called **on yomi**.

この人はイギリス人です。

Kono hito wa Igirisu jin desu.
This person is British.

Kanji 人 means *person*

On reading: **jin**
Kun reading: **hito**

わたしは　ロバートです。

I am Robert.

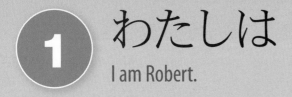

In this unit you will learn to:

- ✓ Use basic Japanese sentence structure.
- ✓ Talk about occupation, nationality and family.
- ✓ Express *this* and *that*.
- ✓ Use Japanese numbers and the counter for people.
- ✓ Recognize the kanji for *I, sun, moon, book/origin* and *person*.

CEFR: Can understand sentences and frequently used expressions related to areas of most immediate relevance, basic personal or family info (A2); Can write about everyday aspects of his environment (people, places, job) (A2).

Meaning and usage

Simple sentence structure with *be*

Using this sentence structure, a topic is introduced by the topic marker は (wa), and then a comment or description of that topic is followed by です (desu). です (desu) is the equivalent of *to be* (am/is/are) in English. The negative of です (desu) is では　ありません (dewa arimasen), 、じゃ　ありません (ja arimasen) or じゃ　ないです (ja nai desu).

The three negative forms above differ in terms of politeness, with では　ありません *being the most formal and* じゃ　ないです *being the least formal.*

わたしは　ロバートです。
Watashi wa Robāto desu.
I am Robert.

ロバートさんは　かいしゃいんです。
Robāto-san wa kaishain desu.
Robert is a company employee.

The topic marker is written as は **(ha)**, *but it is pronounced 'wa'.*

ロバートさんは　イギリスじんですか。
Robāto-san wa igirisu-jin desu ka.
Is Robert English? (Robert, are you English?)

This sentence can be a question to a third person, or to Robert himself, meaning *Robert, are you English?* The particle か **(ka)** at the end of a sentence signifies that it is a question.

はい、イギリスじんです。
Hai, igirisu-jin desu.
Yes, he is English. (Yes I am English.)

いいえ、イギリスじんじゃ　ありません。
Iie, igirisu-jin ja arimasen.
No, he is not English. (No I am not English.)

ロバートさんの　かぞくは　5にんです。
Robāto-san no kazoku wa go-nin desu.
Robert's family is five people. (There are five in Robert's family.)

これは　フランスの　ワインです。
Kore wa furansu no wain desu.
This is French wine.

> さん **(san)** *is equivalent of Mr,*
> *Mrs, Miss, Ms, etc.* ちゃん **(chan)** *is*
> *added to names of little children*
> *and girls, while* くん **(kun)** *is used*
> *for boys and young males.*

The particle の **(no)** is a possessive marker, the equivalent of a possessive apostrophe
('s) in English. It is inserted between two nouns to show some type of ownership or
belonging. The second noun 'belongs' to the first.

あれは　なんですか。
Are wa nan desu ka.
What is that (over there)?

あの　ひとは　だれですか。
Ano hito wa dare desu ka.
Who is that person (over there)?

A Translate the sentences.

1 *I am a company employee.* わたしは　かいしゃいんで
す。**(Watashi wa kaishain desu)**

2 *Mrs Tanaka is a civil servant.* たなかさんこうむいん

3 *Robert is not a student.* ロバートがくせいじゃありません
すぎさんかんごじ

4 *Miss Suzuki is not a nurse.* すずきさんかんごしじゃありません

5 *Mr Yamada is a teacher.* やまだんはきょうしです

6 *Anne (An) is a doctor.* あんはいしゃです

7 *Mr Satō is a bank worker.* さとうんはぎんこういんです

Occupations	
わたし **(watashi)**	*I*
かいしゃいん **(kaishain)**	*company employee*
こうむいん **(kōmuin)**	*civil servant*
ぎんこういん **(ginkōin)**	*bank worker*
きょうし **(kyōshi)**	*teacher*
がくせい **(gakusei)**	*student*
いしゃ **(isha)**	*doctor*
かんごし **(kangoshi)**	*nurse*

> *Remember you can write the answers in the exercises*
> *using Kana and Kanji or transliteration depending on*
> *how confident you feel.*

Countries, nationalities and languages

Here are some common nationalities in Japanese. Note that the names of non-Asian countries are usually written in katakana.

にほん **(Nihon)**	*Japan*
イギリス **(Igirisu)**	*England*
フランス **(Furansu)**	*France*
ドイツ **(Doitsu)**	*Germany*
スペイン **(Supein)**	*Spain*
イタリア **(Itaria)**	*Italy*
アメリカ **(Amerika)**	*America*
ちゅうごく **(Chūgoku)**	*China*
かんこく **(Kankoku)**	*Korea*

In English the words for nationalities, languages and the adjective to describe the origin of something are the same. But in Japanese there are three separate words. For example, the English word *French* has three possible forms in Japanese:

 English language is not イギリスご **(Igirisu-go)**. *It is called* えいご **(eigo)**.

フランスじん	**(Furansu-jin)**	*French (nationality)*
フランスご	**(Furansu-go)**	*French (language)*
フランスの	**(Furansu no)**	*French (origin, e.g. French wine)*

 Remember, the particle の **(no)** signifies ownership or belonging.

B Complete the table.

Nationality	Language	Origin of items
にほんじん (Nihon-jin)	にほんご	にほんの
スペインじん	スペインご (Supein-go)	スペインの
アメリカじん	アメリカご	アメリカの (Amerika no)
ちゅうごくじん	ちゅうごくご (Chūgoku-go)	ちゅうごくの
ドイツじん (Doitsu-jin)	ドイツご	ドイツの
イギリスじん (Igirisu-jin)	えいご (Eigo)	イギリスの
イタリアじん	イタリアご	イタリアの (Itaria no)
かんこくじん	かんこくご	かんこくの (Kankoku no)
フランスじん (Furansu-jin)	フランスじん	フランスの

How to express *this* and *that* in Japanese

This and *that* are called demonstratives. There are three types of *this* and *that* in Japanese, これ (**kore**), それ (**sore**) and あれ (**are**), which correspond to *this one*, *that one* and *that one over there*. これ (**kore**) refers to items near the speaker, それ (**sore**) refers to items near the listener and あれ (**are**) refers to items that are far away from both.

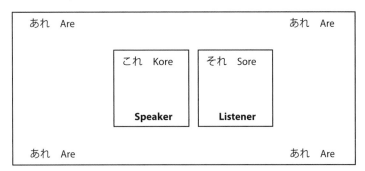

The Japanese demonstratives change their forms in different positions. When これ (**kore**) それ (**sore**) and あれ (**are**) are followed by a noun (for example, *this wine, that wine*, etc.), they become この (**kono**) その (**sono**) and あの (**ano**) respectively.

これは　フランスの　ワインです。
Kore wa Furansu no wain desu.
This is French wine.

この　ワインは　フランスのです。
Kono wain wa Furansu no desu.
This wine is French.

それは　わたしの　けいたいです。
Sore wa watashi no kētai desu.
That one is my mobile phone.

その　けいたいは　わたしのです。
Sono kētai wa watashi no desu.
That mobile phone is mine.

あれは　なんですか。
Are wa nan desu ka.
What is that one over there?

あの　ひとは　だれですか。
Ano hito wa dare desu ka.
Who is that person?

C   Choose the correct words to complete the sentences.

   1 (これ | この)は　(かんこくの | かんこくじん)コンピューターです。
   (Kore/kono) wa (Kankoku no/Kankoku-jin) konpyūtā desu.
   This is a Korean computer.

   2 (それ | その)は　なんですか。
   (Sore/sono) wa nan desu ka.
   What is that?

3 (これ | この)ひとは　だれですか。
(Kore/kono) hito wa dare desu ka.
Who is this person?

4 (あれ | あの)ひとは　（フランスじん | フランスご）です。
(Are/ano) hito wa (Furansu-jin/Furansu-go) desu.
That person is French.

5 (それ | その)は　（ドイツご | ドイツの)とけいです。
(Sore/sono) wa (Doitsu-go/Doitsu no) tokei desu.
That is a German watch.

6 (これ | この)くるまは　（にほんの | にほんご)くるまです。
(Kore/kono) kuruma wa (Nihon no/Nihongo)
kuruma desu.
This car is a Japanese car.

なん (nan)	*what*
だれ (dare)	*who*
わたしの (watashi no)	*my/mine*
ワイン (wain)	*wine*
けいたい (kētai)	*mobile phone*
ひと (hito)	*person*
コンピューター (konpyūtā)	*computer*
とけい (tokei)	*watch/clock*
くるま (kuruma)	*car*

Vocabulary

Words for family

There are two sets of words for family – words for your own family, and words for other people's families.

English	My family	Other people's families
father	ちち (chichi)	おとうさん (otōsan)
mother	はは (haha)	おかあさん (okāsan)
son	むすこ (musuko)	むすこさん (musuko-san)
daughter	むすめ (musume)	むすめさん (musume-san)
husband	しゅじん (shujin)/おっと (otto)	ごしゅじん (go-shujin)
wife	つま (tsuma)/かない (kanai)	おくさん (okusan)
siblings	きょうだい (kyōdai)	ごきょうだい (go- kyōdai)
family	かぞく (kazoku)	ごかぞく (go-kazoku)

D Put the words in the correct order to form sentences.

1 は | かいしゃいん | か | ロバートさん | です (wa/kaishain/ka/Robāto-san/desu)
ロバートさんは　かいしゃいんですか。 (Robāto-san wa kaishain desu ka)

2 きょうし | ちち | です | は (kyōshi/chichi/desu/wa)
ちちはきょうしです

3 です | は | とけい | はは | の | これ (desu/wa/tokei/haha/no/kore)
はははこれのとけいです

4 ひと | ごしゅじん | は | あの | すずきさん | です | の (hito/go-shujin/wa/ano/Suzuki-san/desu/no)

すずきさんごのごしゅじんはあので す

5 は | がくせい | です | むすこさん | か (wa/gakusei/desu/musuko-san/ka)

むすこさん はがくせいで すか

6 の | たなかさん | です | おくさん | は | イギリスじん (no/Tanaka-san/desu/okusan/wa/Igirisu-jin)

たなかさんのおくさんは イギリスじんで す

Vocabulary

Numbers

The Japanese numbers:

0	**zero/rei**	ゼロ・れい	7	**nana/shichi**	なな/しち
1	**ichi**	いち	8	**hachi**	はち
2	**ni**	に	9	**kyū/ku**	きゅう/く
3	**san**	さん	10	**jū**	じゅう
4	**yon/yo/shi**	よん/よ/し	11	**jūichi**	じゅういち
5	**go**	ご	12	**jūni**	じゅうに
6	**roku**	ろく	20	**nijū**	にじゅう

30, 40, 50, etc. are simply 'three ten' さんじゅう (**sanjū**), 'four ten' よんじゅう (**yonjū**), 'five ten' ごじゅう (**gojū**), etc.

In order to express how many people you have in your family, you need to add the *counter* for counting people. The counter for people is 〜にん (**nin**), which is added to the numbers except for one person ひとり (**hitori**) and two people ふたり (**futari**). When you want to ask 'how many people', the question word is なんにん (**nan-nin**).

ごかぞくは　なんにんですか。
go-kazoku wa nan-nin desu ka.
How many people are there in your family?

わたしの　かぞくは　よにんです。
Watashi no kazoku wa yo-nin desu.
My family is four. (There are four people in my family.)

 Remember there are two sets of words for family. Look back at the table. When asking about another person's family you use the words for 'other people's families'.

How to count people

1	hitori	ひとり	7	nana-nin/shichi-nin	ななにん/しちにん	
2	futari	ふたり	8	hachi-nin	はちにん	
3	san-nin	さんにん	9	kyū-nin	きゅうにん	
4	yo-nin	よにん	10	jū-nin	じゅうにん	
5	go-nin	ごにん	11	jūichi-nin	じゅういちにん	
6	roku-nin	ろくにん	12	jūni-nin	じゅうににん	

📖 Reading

E   Read the dialogue and answer the questions.

ロバート: はじめまして。わたしは　ロバート・ジョーンズです。イギリスじんです。

たなか: はじめまして。わたしは　たなかです。ロバートさん、おしごとは?

ロバート: かいしゃいんです。

たなか: わたしも　かいしゃいんです。ごかぞくは　なんにんですか。

ロバート: わたしの　かぞくは　よにんです。つまと、むすこが　ふたりと、わたしです。つまは
ぎんこういんです。

はじめまして (hajimemashite)	*how do you do*
おしごとは (o-shigoto wa)	*what's your job (lit. your job?)*
～も (mo)	*also*
～と (to)	*and/with*

Robert: Hajimemashite. Watashi wa Robāto Jōnzu desu. Igirisu-jin desu.

Tanaka: Hajimemashite. Watashi wa Tanaka desu. Robāto-san, O-shigoto wa?

Robert: Kaishain desu.

Tanaka: Watashi mo kaishain desu. Go-kazoku wa nan-nin desuka?

Robert: Watashi no kazoku wa yo-nin desu. Tsuma to musuko ga futari to watashi desu. Tsuma
wa ginkōin desu.

1 What is Robert's nationality?

BRITISH

2 What is Mr Tanaka's occupation?

CONPANY EMPLOYEE

3 What is Robert's wife's occupation?

BANKWORKER

4 How many children does Robert have?

2

F For each group of words, identify the odd one out.

1 かいしゃいん | ぎんこういん | がくせい | わたし

2 イギリス | にほんじん | フランス | かんこく

3 コンピューター | とけい | ワイン | けいたい

4 ちち | はは | かぞく | ごしゅじん

5 ふたり | ごにん | じゅうに | ひとり

Don't forget to write down new vocabulary so that you can revise and memorize it easily.

 # Writing

G Write a short paragraph introducing yourself. Make sure to mention your nationality, occupation and family.

わたしのかぞくは
きょうだいふたりですとははとちち。
わたしはアメリカでです
ありがとう

Japanese script

We will introduce the following five kanji in this unit.

Kanji	Reading	Meaning	Example words
私	わたし、し (watashi/shi)	I	<ruby>私<rt>わたし</rt></ruby>
日	に、にち、ひ、び (ni/nichi/hi/bi)	sun, day	15<ruby>日<rt>にち</rt></ruby> (15th) <ruby>日<rt>にち</rt></ruby>よう<ruby>日<rt>び</rt></ruby> (Sunday)
月	つき、げつ、がつ (tsuki/getsu/gatsu)	moon, month	5<ruby>月<rt>がつ</rt></ruby> (May) <ruby>月<rt>げつ</rt></ruby>よう<ruby>日<rt>び</rt></ruby>、 (Monday)
本	ほん、ぽん、ぼん (hon/pon/bon)	origin, book, a counter for thin and long objects	<ruby>日本<rt>にほん</rt></ruby>
人	ひと、じん、にん (hito/jin/nin)	person, people	<ruby>日本人<rt>にほんじん</rt></ruby>、イギリス<ruby>人<rt>じん</rt></ruby>、4<ruby>人<rt>にん</rt></ruby>、 あの<ruby>人<rt>ひと</rt></ruby>

H Choose the correct kanji from the box to complete the sentences.

日本	<ruby>人<rt>にん</rt></ruby>	日よう日	月	<ruby>人<rt>ひと</rt></ruby>	日本人	日	私	<ruby>人<rt>じん</rt></ruby>

1 たなかさんは 日本人 です。

2 ロバートさんは　イギリス 人 です。

3 あれは　本　の　くるまです。

4 本　の　かぞくは　4日　です。

5 あの 日　は　だれですか。

6 5 日 15月　は　本　です。

Remember, the pronunciation of a kanji changes depending on the context in which it is used!

Self-check

Tick the box which matches your level of confidence.

1 = very confident   2 = need more practice   3 = not confident

下のボックスにじしんがあるかないかチェックしましょう。
    1. じしんがある   2. れんしゅうがひつよう   3. じしんがない

	1	2	3
Using basic Japanese sentence structure.	✓		
Talking about occupation, nationality and family.	✓		
Expressing *this* and *that*.	✓		
Using Japanese numbers and the counter for people.	✓		
Recognizing the kanji for *I, sun, moon, book/origin* and *person*.	✓		

* For more information on occupation, nationality and family, and how to express *this* and *that* refer to *Complete Japanese,* Unit 1, or *Get Started In Japanese,* Units 1–5.

2

まいあさ　コーヒーを　のみます。

I drink coffee every morning.

In this unit you will learn to:

✅ Use the Japanese present tense (masu form).

✅ Use Japanese particles in the correct way.

✅ Invite others to do something and make suggestions.

✅ Talk about daily routines and future actions.

✅ Recognize the kanji for *fire, water, wood, gold* and *soil*.

CEFR: Can understand texts that consist mainly of high frequency everyday or job-related language (B1); Can make and respond to invitations, suggestions and apologies (A2); Can describe plans, arrangements, habits and routines, past activities and personal experiences (A2).

Meaning and usage

Present tense

The ます form (masu form) in Japanese is a present tense which is used as follows:

1   to express actions which are repeated regularly (habitual actions):

7じに　おきます。
Shichi-ji ni okimasu.
(I) wake up at 7 o'clock.

まいあさ　コーヒーを　のみます。
Maiasa kōhī o nomimasu.
(I) drink coffee every morning.

私は　にくは　たべません。
Watashi wa niku 'wa' tabemasen
I don't eat meat.

The particle を (o) marks the object of a sentence. Notice it is pronounced 'o' but spelt as 'wo'. It is often replaced with 'wa' in negative sentences as above, **Watashi wa niku _wa_ tabemasen**. To form the negative, replace ます (**masu**) with ません (**masen**).

2 to express future actions:

<ruby>日<rt>にち</rt></ruby>よう<ruby>日<rt>び</rt></ruby>に　なにを　しますか。

Nichiyōbi ni nani o shimasu ka.

What are you doing on Sunday?

らいしゅう　<ruby>日本<rt>にほん</rt></ruby>へ　いきます。

Raishū Nihon e ikimasu.

(I) will go to Japan next week.

The particle へ (e) is attached after the place noun, *nihon*, meaning *to*. Notice it is pronounced 'e' but spelt as 'he'.

Vocabulary

Verbs in ます (masu) form

おきます okimasu	*wake up*	たべます tabemasu	*eat*
ねます nemasu	*sleep*	のみます nomimasu	*drink*
はたらきます hatarakimasu	*work*	みます mimasu	*see, watch*
いきます ikimasu	*go*	ききます kikimasu	*listen*
きます kimasu	*come*	よみます yomimasu	*read*
かえります kaerimasu	*return*	かきます kakimasu	*write*
します shimasu	*do, play (sports)*	べんきょうします benkyōshimasu	*study*

Everyday items

A **Complete the sentences using the vocabulary in the box. You will also need to select the right particle.**

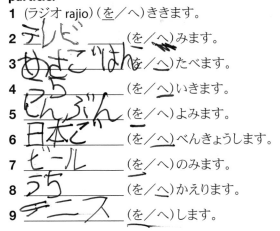

1 (ラジオ rajio)（<u>を</u>／へ）ききます。

2 テレビ_____（を／へ）みます。

3 あさごはん（を／へ）たべます。

4 うち_____（を／へ）いきます。

5 しんぶん_____（を／へ）よみます。

6 日本ご_____（を／<u>へ</u>）べんきょうします。

7 ビール_____（を／へ）のみます。

8 うち_____（を／<u>へ</u>）かえります。

9 テニス_____（を／へ）します。

あさごはん (asa gohan)	*breakfast*
ビール (bīru)	*beer*
ラジオ (rajio)	*radio*
テレビ (terebi)	*TV*
<ruby>日本<rt>にほん</rt></ruby>ご (Nihon-go)	*Japanese language*
テニス (tenisu)	*tennis*
しんぶん (shinbun)	*newspaper*
かいしゃ (kaisha)	*office, company*
うち (uchi)	*home*

The particles: へ (e) and で (de)

The particle へ (e) is attached to place nouns to describe movement towards them, while the particle で (de) is attached to place nouns when actions or events take place there.

1 8じに　かいしゃへ　いきます。
Hachi-ji ni kaisha e ikimasu.
I go to work at 8.

2 9じから　5じまで　かいしゃで　はたらきます。
Ku-ji kara go-ji made kaisha de hatarakimasu.
I work in the office from 9 to 5.

3 7じに　うちへ　かえります。
Shichi-ji ni uchi e kaerimasu.
I return home (go home) at 7.

4 うちで　ともだちと　テレビを　みます。
Uchi de tomodachi to terebi o mimasu.
I watch TV with my friend at home.

～じ (～ ji)	～ o'clock (note: 4 じ (yo-ji), 7 じ (shichi-ji), 9 じ (ku-ji))
～に (～ ni)	at (～ o'clock)
～から～まで (～ kara ～ made)	from ～ to ～
～と (～ to)	with ～ e.g. かぞくと (kazoku to) with my family
ともだち (tomodachi)	friend(s)

Places and free time

B **Choose either で (de) or へ (e) to complete the sentences.**

1 イギリス (<u>で</u>／へ)かえります。

2 ぎんこう (で／<u>へ</u>)いきます。

3 レストラン(<u>で</u>／へ)ひるごはんを　たべます。

4 びじゅつかん (で／<u>へ</u>)きます。

5 8じに　がっこう(で／<u>へ</u>)いきます。

6 がっこう(<u>で</u>／へ)べんきょうします。

7 ともだちと　えいがかん(<u>で</u>／へ)えいがを　みます。

8 かいしゃ(<u>で</u>／へ)メイルを　よみます。

レストラン (resutoran)	restaurant
ぎんこう (ginkō)	bank
えいがかん (eigakan)	cinema
びじゅつかん (bijutsukan)	art gallery
がっこう (gakkō)	school
えいが (eiga)	film
ひるごはん (hiru gohan)	lunch
メイル (mēru)	email

The particles: に (ni)

The particle に (ni) has many functions. In this unit, we will focus on its use in time expressions. に (ni) is attached to specific time expressions such as days of week (e.g. *Monday*), dates (*15th May*), years (e.g. *2014*), and times (e.g. *3 o'clock*) to mean *on* (such as *on Monday*) or *at* (e.g. *at 3 o'clock*). It is not attached to relative time expressions, such as *today*, *next week* or *every day*.

Days of the week

Here are the days of the week and other common ways to express time for habitual actions linked to the present tense.

月ようび (getsuyōbi)	Monday
かよう日 (kayōbi)	Tuesday
すいよう日 (suiyōbi)	Wednesday
もくよう日 (mokuyōbi)	Thursday
きんよう日 (kinyōbi)	Friday
どよう日 (doyōbi)	Saturday
日よう日 (nichiyōbi)	Sunday
きょう (kyō)	today
あした (ashita)	tomorrow
こんしゅう (konshū)	this week
らいしゅう (raishū)	next week
まい日 (mainichi)	every day
まいばん (maiban)	every night

> 🍎 Note that the kanji 日 has several readings (pronunciations). よう日 (yōbi) stands for days of the week.

C Choose either に (ni) or × (no particle needed) to complete the sentences.

1 もくよう日 __に__ ともだちと えいがを みます。

2 きょう __に__ 7じ __に__ うちへ　かえります。

3 日よう日 __に__ びじゅつかんへ　いきます。

4 まいばん __に__ 12じ __に__ ねます。

5 まい日 __に__ 9じから ＿＿＿＿＿5じまで
＿＿＿＿＿ はたらきます。

6 らいしゅう＿＿＿＿＿ 日本へ　いきます。

A SHORT SUMMARY OF THE PARTICLES SO FAR	
は (wa)	marks the topic (often the subject) of the sentence.
Tanaka san *wa* asagohan o tabemasu – *Mr Tanaka eats breakfast*	
を (o)	marks the object of the sentence.
Tanaka san wa **asagohan *o*** tabemasu – *Mr Tanaka eats breakfast*	
へ (e)	means *to* with verbs of movement.
Nihon *e* ikimasu – *I go to Japan*	
で (de)	marks the place where an action happens.
Uchi *de* eiga o mimasu – *I watch a film at home*	
に (ni)	means *on, in, at* when used with time expressions.
5ji *ni* – *at 5 o'clock*	
と (to)	means *and, with*.
Chichi *to* terebi o mimasu – *I watch TV with my father*	
から (kara)	means *from*.
5ji *kara* – *from 5 o'clock*	
まで (made)	means *to, until*.
5ji *made* – *until 5 o'clock*	

**D Choose the correct particles from the box to complete the sentences.
Use x if no particle is needed.**

は	を	へ	で	に	と	から	まで

1 私 <u>は</u> すいよう日 <u>に</u> ともだち <u>と</u> テニス
<u>を</u> します。

2 がっこう <u>は</u> 日本ご <u>に</u> べんきょうします。

3 まい日 <u>は</u> ラジオ <u>へ</u> ききます。

4 あした <u>は</u> アメリカ <u>へ</u> いきます。

5 まいばん <u>は</u> 11じ <u>へ</u> ねます。

6 かいしゃ <u>は</u> 9じ <u>は</u> 5じ <u>に</u> はたらきます。

～ませんか (masen ka) and ～ましょう (mashō)

If you want to invite others to do something, you can change ～ます to ～ませんか (masen ka). This form is used when the speaker is unsure whether or not others want to join him/her.

If you want to make a suggestion (*shall we?* or *let's*), you change the ～ます part of the verb to ましょう.

Both of these verb forms are often used with いっしょに (**issho ni**), meaning *together*.

E **Use the noun and the correct verb to form pairs of sentences.**

いきます、します、たべます、のみます、みます

1 ひるごはん (hiru gohan)

   A: いっしょに　ひるごはんを　たべませんか。

   Issho ni hiru gohan o tabemasen ka

   B: はい、たべましょう。

   Hai, tabemashō

2 テニス (tenisu)

   A:

   B:

3 えいが (eiga)

   A:

   B:

4 ビール (bīru)

   A: _____

   B: _____

5 きょうと (Kyōto)

   A: _____

   B: _____

📖 Reading

F Read about Mr Tanaka's daily routine and answer the questions in Japanese.

たなかさんの　まい日

たなかさんは、まいあさ　7じに　おきます。
コーヒーを　のみます。あさごはんは　たべません。
8じに　かいしゃへ　いきます。9じから　5じまで
はたらきます。いつも　かいしゃで　ひるごはんを
たべます。6じに　うちへ　かえります。
7じに　ばんごはんを　たべます。それから
テレビを　みます。ときどき　ブログを　かきます。
11じに　ねます。

ばんごはん (ban gohan)	dinner
それから (sorekara)	and then
ブログ (burogu)	blog

Tanaka-san no mainichi

Tanaka-san wa maiasa shichi-ji ni okimasu. Kōhī o nomimasu. Asa gohan wa tabemasen. Hachi-ji ni kaisha e ikimasu. Ku-ji kara go-ji made hatarakimasu. Itsumo kaisha de hiru gohan o tabemasu. Roku-ji ni uchi e kaerimasu. Shichi-ji ni ban gohan o tabemasu. Sorekara terebi o mimasu. Tokidoki burogu o kakimasu. Jūichi-ji ni nemasu.

1 What time does Tanaka-san get up?

_____

2 Does he have breakfast?

_____

3 Where does he always have lunch?

_____

4 What does he do after dinner?

_____

5 What does he sometimes do before going to bed?

_____

Vocabulary

Expressions of frequency

The present tense is often used with expressions which indicate how often actions take place.

いつも (itsumo)	*always*
たいてい (taitei)	*usually*
よく (yoku)	*often*
ときどき (tokidoki)	*sometimes*
あまり ～ません (amari ～masen)	*not very often* (with the negative verb form)
ぜんぜん ～ません (zenzen ～masen)	*not at all* (with the negative verb form)

G Translate the sentences. Use the expressions of frequency to help you.

1 *I always have my lunch in my office.*
　　　わたし
　　　私は　いつも　かいしゃで　ひるごはんを　たべます。

2 *I don't read newspapers very often.*
　　　わたし
　　　私は　あまり　しんぶんを　よみません。

3 *I often drink beer with my friends.*

_____

4 *Mr Tanaka doesn't watch TV very often.*

_____

5 *I don't listen to radio at all.*

_____

6 *I usually watch films at home.*

_____

7 *Robert sometimes works until 8 o'clock.*

_____

H **For each group of words, identify the odd one out.**

1 かいしゃ | うち | がっこう | きょう

2 たべます | かえります | みます | よみます

3 ぎんこう | あした | らいしゅう | まいあさ

4 しんぶん | 日本ご | テレビ | ラジオ

5 えいがかん | テニス | レストラン | びじゅつかん

📝 Writing

I **Write a short paragraph about your daily routine. Use the description of Mr Tanaka's daily routine on p. 18 to help you. Make sure to mention what time you get up, go to work and eat meals, and what you do during your free time (for example, reading newspapers, watching TV, writing a blog, etc.).**

<table>
<tr><td></td><td></td></tr>
<tr><td></td><td></td></tr>
<tr><td></td><td></td></tr>
<tr><td></td><td></td></tr>
<tr><td></td><td></td></tr>
<tr><td></td><td></td></tr>
<tr><td></td><td></td></tr>
<tr><td></td><td></td></tr>
<tr><td></td><td></td></tr>
<tr><td></td><td></td></tr>
<tr><td></td><td></td></tr>
<tr><td></td><td></td></tr>
<tr><td></td><td></td></tr>
<tr><td></td><td></td></tr>
<tr><td></td><td></td></tr>
<tr><td></td><td></td></tr>
</table>

Japanese script

We will introduce the following five kanji in this unit.

KANJI	READING	MEANING	EXAMPLE WORDS
火	ひ、び、か (hi/bi/ka)	*fire*	火 (*fire*), 火よう日 (*Tuesday*)
水	みず、すい (mizu/sui)	*water*	水 (*water*), 水よう日 (*Wednesday*)
木	き、もく (ki/moku)	*wood, tree*	木 (*tree*), 木よう日 (*Thursday*)
金	かね、きん (kane/kin)	*metal, money, gold*	お金 (*money*), 金よう日 (*Friday*)
土	つち、ど (tsuchi/do)	*soil, earth*	土よう日 (*Saturday*)

J Translate the following sentences into English.

1 月よう日から　金よう日まで　はたらきます。

_____

2 火よう日と　木よう日に　日本ごの　がっこうへ　いきます。

_____

3 水よう日に　テニスを　します。

_____

4 土よう日に　ともだちと　ばんごはんを　たべます。

_____

5 日よう日に　よく　びじゅつかんへ　いきます。

_____

Self-check

Tick the box which matches your level of confidence.

1 = very confident   2 = need more practice   3 = not confident

下のボックスにじしんがあるかないかチェックしましょう。

1. じしんがある   2. れんしゅうがひつよう   3. じしんがない

	1	2	3
Using the Japanese present tense (masu form).			
Using Japanese particles in the correct way.			
Inviting others to do something and making suggestions.			
Talking about daily routines and future actions.			
Expressing how often actions take place.			
Recognizing the kanji for *fire, water, wood, gold* and *soil*.			

* For more information on the masu form, the particles and how to invite others refer to *Complete Japanese,* Unit 2, or *Get Started in Japanese,* Units 8 and 9.

3

こうえんに　おとこの　こが　います。

There is a boy in a park.

> **In this unit you will learn to:**
> ✅ Talk about where things and people are using arimasu, imasu and location words.
> ✅ Express how many people/things there are using Japanese counters.
> ✅ Use Japanese numbers from 100.
> ✅ Recognize the kanji for *man*, *woman*, *child*, *yen* and *inside*.

CEFR: Can understand texts that consist mainly of high frequency everyday or job-related language (B1); Can write about everyday aspects of his environment (people, places, job) (A2); Can handle numbers (A1).

Meaning and usage

The verb あります (arimasu) and います (imasu)

あります **(arimasu)** is a verb that is used to express where non-living, inanimate things are. います **(imasu)**, on the other hand, is used to describe the existence of living, animate things (people and animals). The negative forms are ありません **(arimasen)** and いません **(imasen)** respectively. Both verbs are also used to express possession and relationships, such as having money, time, a husband or wife, children, etc.

1 to express where things/people are:

こうえんに　おとこの　こが　います。
Kōen ni otoko no ko ga imasu.
There is a boy in a park.

こうえんに　木が　あります。
Kōen ni ki ga arimasu.
There is a tree in a park.

The particle が **(ga)** is called the subject marker, and it marks the subject of the sentence.

木の　したに　たなかさんが　います。
Ki no shita ni Tanaka-san ga imasu.
Mr Tanaka is under the tree.

うちに　だれも　いません。
Uchi ni daremo imasen.
There is no one at home.

この　へやに　コンピューターが　にだい　あります。
Kono heya ni konpyūtā ga ni-dai arimasu.
There are two computers in this room.

びじゅつかんは　どこに　ありますか。
Bijutsukan wa doko ni arimasuka.
Where is the art gallery?

ロバートさんは　どこに　いますか。
Robāto-san wa doko ni imasuka.
Where is Robert?

2 to express possession and family relationships:

たなかさんは　お金<ruby>金<rt>かね</rt></ruby>が　あります。
Tanaka-san wa okane ga arimasu.
Mr Tanaka has money.

たなかさんは　おくさんが　います。
Tanaka-san wa okusan ga imasu.
Mr Tanaka has a wife.

 *For these two sentences, the particle は **wa** (the topic marker) is used rather than が **ga** (the subject marker). In these sentences, the speaker raises **bijutsukan** and **Robāto-san** as the topic of conversation, and asks where they are. The topic should be something the speaker assumes the listener already knows.*

How to express *here, there* and *over there*.

There are three ways of saying *this one*, *that one* and *that one over there* in Japanese. There are also three terms for *here*, *there* and *over there* in Japanese. They are, respectively, ここ (**koko**), そこ (**soko**), and あそこ (**asoko**). The Japanese word for *where* is どこ (**doko**).

A Put the words in the correct order to form sentences. Remember to finish sentences with a Japanese full stop (。).

1 こうえん | おとこの　人<ruby>人<rt>ひと</rt></ruby> | います | が | に (**kōen/otoko no hito/imasu/ga/ni**)

_____

2 テレビ | に | あります | いま | が (**terebi/ni/arimasu/ima/ga**)

_____

3 と | ねこ | が | います | にわ | いぬ | に (**to/neko/ga/imasu/niwa/inu/ni**)

_____

4 おんなの　人<ruby>人<rt>ひと</rt></ruby> | に | あそこ | が | います (**onna no hito/ni/asoko/ga/imasu**)

_____

People and places	
おとこの　人<ruby>人<rt>ひと</rt></ruby> (otoko no hito)	man
おんなの　人<ruby>人<rt>ひと</rt></ruby> (onna no hito)	woman
おとこの　こ (otoko no ko)	boy
おんなの　こ (onna no ko)	girl
いぬ (inu)	dog
ねこ (neko)	cat
にわ (niwa)	garden
いま (ima)	living room
へや (heya)	room
こうえん (kōen)	park

5 へや｜あります｜コンピューター｜が｜この｜に (heya/arimasu/konpyūtā/ga/kono/ni)

_____

6 おとこの　こ｜おんなの　こ｜と｜レストラン｜が｜います｜に (otoko no ko/onna no ko/to/resutoran/ga/imasu/ni)

_____

Location words

In English, location words (prepositions) are used to describe where things and people are. In Japanese, we use location words plus the particle に (ni). In Japanese you say the point of reference/place of location plus の (no) first, followed by the location word plus に (ni).

木の　したに　たなかさんが　います。
Ki no shita ni Tanaka-san ga imasu.
Mr Tanaka is under the tree.

れいぞうこの　なかに　ビールが　あります。
Reizōko no naka ni bīru ga arimasu.
There is a beer in the fridge.

うえ (ue)	above, on
した (shita)	under
なか (naka)	in, inside
まえ (mae)	in front of
うしろ (ushiro)	behind
よこ (yoko)	side, next to
ちかく (chikaku)	near

と (to) and や (ya)

Nouns can be combined by using the particle や (ya). While と (to) combines nouns, や (ya) denotes that the nouns are representatives of a larger group, i.e., there may be some more things in the group. Often など (nado) is added to signify there are other things/people.

こうえんに　いぬと　ねこが　います。
Kōen ni inu to neko ga imasu.
There is a dog and a cat in the park (nothing else).

こうえんに　いぬや　ねこ(など)が　います。
Kōen ni inu ya neko (nado) ga imasu.
There is a dog and a cat (among other things) in the park.

> There is no distinction between singular and plural in Japanese, so the sentences could mean There are dogs and cats (nothing else/among other things) in the park *as well.*

B   Translate the sentences.

1 *There are some beers in the fridge.*

れいぞうこの　なかに　ビールが　あります。**(reizōko no naka ni bīru ga arimasu.)**

2 *There is a mobile phone and a watch and so on in this bag.*

_____

3 *There is a bookshop next to the department store.*

_____

4 *There is a pair of shoes in this box.*

_____

5 *There is a vending machine in front of the station.*

_____

6 *There is a book on that desk.*

_____

7 *There is a boy and a girl under that tree over there.*

_____

8 *There is a bank near the station.*

_____

き 木 **(ki)**	tree
つくえ **(tsukue)**	desk
はこ **(hako)**	box
れいぞうこ **(reizōko)**	fridge
えき **(eki)**	station
ドア **(doa)**	door
デパート **(depāto)**	department store
かばん **(kaban)**	bag
くつ **(kutsu)**	shoes
ほん 本 **(hon)**	book
ほん 本や **(honya)**	bookshop
じどうはんばいき **(jidōhanbaiki)**	vending machine
ビール **(bīru)**	beer

How to count objects/people

In Japanese, there is a set of words called *counters*, which are used for counting objects/people. They are similar to *slices* and *bars* in *two slices of toast* and *three bars of chocolate*. It is necessary to know the counters for each object.

この　へやに　コンピューターが　にだい　あります。
Kono heya ni konpyūtā ga ni-dai arimasu.
There are two computers in this room.

だい **(dai)** is the counter for machines and vehicles and it follows the number two (に **(ni)**). The numbers and counters *follow* the subject コンピューター **(konpyūtā)** and the subject marker が **(ga)**.

Here are some useful counters:

	Machines and vehicles 〜だい	Thin and flat things 〜まい	Thin and long things 〜ほん(本)	Other small objects	People 〜にん(人)	Small animals 〜ひき
1	いちだい ichi-dai	いちまい ichi-mai	いっぽん ippon	ひとつ hitotsu	ひとり hitori	いっぴき ippiki
2	にだい ni-dai	にまい ni-mai	にほん ni-hon	ふたつ futatsu	ふたり futari	にひき ni-hiki
3	さんだい san-dai	さんまい san-mai	さんぼん san-bon	みっつ mittsu	さんにん san-nin	さんびき san-biki
4	よんだい yon-dai	よんまい yon-mai	よんほん yon-hon	よっつ yottsu	よにん yo-nin	よんひき yon-hiki
5	ごだい go-dai	ごまい go-mai	ごほん go-hon	いつつ itsutsu	ごにん go-nin	ごひき go-hiki
6	ろくだい roku-dai	ろくまい roku-mai	ろっぽん roppon	むっつ muttsu	ろくにん roku-nin	ろっぴき roppiki
7	ななだい nana-dai	ななまい nana-mai	ななほん nana-hon	ななつ nanatsu	ななにん/しちにん nana-nin/shichi-nin	ななひき nana-hiki
8	はちだい hachi-dai	はちまい hachi-mai	はっぽん happon	やっつ yattsu	はちにん hachi-nin	はっぴき happiki
9	きゅうだい kyū-dai	きゅうまい kyū-mai	きゅうほん kyū-hon	ここのつ kokonotsu	きゅうにん kyū-nin	きゅうひき kyū-hiki
10	じゅうだい jū-dai	じゅうまい jū-mai	じゅっぽん juppon	とお tō	じゅうにん jū-nin	じゅっぴき juppiki
Question form	なんだい nan-dai	なんまい nan-mai	なんぼん nan-bon	いくつ ikutsu	なんにん nan-nin	なんびき nan-biki

The pronunciation of a number or counter sometimes changes with some counters. The numbers that often trigger changes are 1, 3, 6, 8 and 10.

C **Complete the sentences by choosing the correct counters.**

1 あそこに　おとこの　こが　（ふたり (**futari**) 2）　います。

2 れいぞうこに　ビールが　_____　8　あります。

3 にわに　いぬが　_____　3　います。

4 えきの　まえに　くるまが　_____　2　あります。

5 つくえの　うえに　りんごが　_____　7　あります。

6 はこの　なかに　きってが　_____　6　あります。

7 がっこうに　がくせいが　_____　5　います。

りんご (**ringo**)	*apple*
きって (**kitte**)	*postal stamps*

なにも (nanimo) and だれも (daremo)

なに (**nani**) and だれ (**dare**) are question words, meaning *what* and *who* respectively. In order to say *there is nothing* and *there is no one*, the particle も (**mo**) is attached and the negative form of the verb is used.

れいぞうこに　なにが　ありますか。
Reizōko ni nani ga ariamsu ka.
What's in the fridge?

れいぞうこに　なにも　ありません。
Reizōko ni nanimo ariamsen.
There is nothing in the fridge.

D **Complete the dialogues with the correct particles. Use x if no particle is needed.**

1 たなかさん: この(x)はこ(の) なか (に) なに (が) ありますか。

ロバートさん: ほん _____ けいたい _____ とけいなど
_____ あります。

2 ロバートさん: ほんやは　どこ _____ ありますか。

すずきさん: デパート _____ うしろ _____ あります。

3 たなかさん: こうえん _____ だれ _____ いますか。

すずきさん: だれ _____ いません。

4 すずきさん: あの _____ つくえ _____ うえ _____ なに
_____ ありますか。

ロバートさん: コンピューター _____ 2だい _____ あります。

E **Complete the dialogue between Robert and Mr Tanaka using the words in the box.**

ロバート:　たなかさん、土よう日に　えいがを　いっしょに　みませんか。
　　　　　_____ が　2まい　あります。

たなか:	土よう日は、＿＿＿＿＿＿ が あります。かいしゃで はたらきます。						

たなか: 土よう日は、＿＿＿＿＿＿ が あります。
かいしゃで はたらきます。

ロバート: 日よう日は どうですか?

たなか: 日よう日は ともだちと ＿＿＿＿＿＿
が あります。こうえんで テニスを
します。

ロバート: ざんねんですね。

たなか: でも、らいしゅうの 土よう日は
＿＿＿＿＿＿ が あります。

ロバート: そうですか。じゃ、らいしゅうの
土よう日に いきましょう。

お金 (okane)	money
じかん (jikan)	time
しごと (shigoto)	work
やくそく (yakusoku)	appointment (informal)
チケット (chiketto)	ticket
どう (dō)	how, how about
ざんねんですね (zannen desu ne)	it's a shame
じゃ (ja)	well then

Vocabulary

Numbers from 100

Familiarize yourself with the Japanese numbers.

100	ひゃく **hyaku**	1,000	せん **sen**	10,000	いちまん **ichiman**		
200	にひゃく **nihyaku**	2,000	にせん **nisen**	20,000	にまん **niman**		
300	さんびゃく **sanbyaku**	3,000	さんぜん **sanzen**	30,000	さんまん **sanman**		
400	よんひゃく **yonhyaku**	4,000	よんせん **yonsen**	40,000	よんまん **yonman**		
500	ごひゃく **gohyaku**	5,000	ごせん **gosen**	50,000	ごまん **goman**		
600	ろっぴゃく **roppyaku**	6,000	ろくせん **rokusen**	60,000	ろくまん **rokuman**		
700	ななひゃく **nanahyaku**	7,000	ななせん **nanasen**	70,000	ななまん **nanaman**		
800	はっぴゃく **happyaku**	8,000	はっせん **hassen**	80,000	はちまん **hachiman**		
900	きゅうひゃく **kyūhyaku**	9,000	きゅうせん **kyūsen**	90,000	きゅうまん **kyūman**		

100,000 is じゅうまん **(jūman)**, *1,000,000 is* ひゃくまん **(hyakuman)**, *10,000,000 is* せんまん **(senman)** *and 100,000,000 is* いちおく **(ichioku)**, *etc. How much is it in Japanese is* (それは)いくらですか **(sore wa ikura desu ka)**

F   Convert the numbers into Japanese.

1 *2,350*   にせんさんびゃくごじゅう **(nisen sanbyaku gojū)**

2 *3,600*   _____

3 *642*   _____

4 *79,200*   _____

5 *18,800*   _____

6 *510*   _____

7 *52,167*   _____

 Reading

G   Read the dialogue and answer the questions in Japanese.

ロバート：   すみません、この　ちかくに
                    デパートが　ありますか。

おんなのひと人：   はい、あります。あそこに　えきが
                    ありますね。デパートは、あの
                    えきの　まえに　あります。

ロバート：   ありがとう　ございます。

ロバート：   すみません、ネクタイは　ありますか。

てんいん：   はい、あります。こちらです。

ロバート：   この　ネクタイは　いくらですか。

てんいん：   それは　8,000えんです。それは
                    イタリアの　ネクタイです。

ロバート：   この　ネクタイは　いくらですか。

てんいん：   5,000えんです。フランスの　ネクタイです。

ロバート：   じゃ、フランスの　ネクタイを　ください。

すみません **(sumimasen)**	*excuse me*
この　ちかく **(kono chikaku)**	*near here*
ありがとう　ございます **(arigatō gozaimasu)**	*thank you very much*
ネクタイ **(nekutai)**	*tie*
てんいん **(ten-in)**	*shop assistant*
こちら **(kochira)**	*this way*
いくら **(ikura)**	*how much*
〜えん **(en)**	*yen*
〜を　ください **(〜o kudasai)**	*please give me 〜*

Robāto: Sumimasen, kono chikaku ni depāto ga arimasuka.

Onna no hito: Hai, arimasu. Asoko ni eki ga arimasu ne. Depāto wa ano eki no

               mae ni arimasu.

Robāto: Arigatō gozaimasu.

Robāto:	Sumimasen, nekutai wa arimasu ka.
Ten-in:	Hai, arimasu. Kochira desu.
Robāto:	Kono nekutai wa ikura desu ka.
Ten-in:	Sore wa 8,000-en desu. Sore wa Itaria no nekutai desu.
Robāto:	Kono nekutai wa ikura desu ka.
Ten-in:	5,000-en desu. Furansu no nekutai desu.
Robāto:	Ja, Furansu no nekutai o kudasai.

1 ロバートさんは　どこへ　いきますか。(Robāto-san wa doko e ikimasu ka)

_____

2 デパートは　どこに　ありますか。(depāto wa doko ni arimasu ka)

_____

3 イタリアの　ネクタイは　いくらですか。 (Itaria no nekutai wa ikura desu ka)

_____

4 フランスの　ネクタイは　いくらですか。(Furansu no nekutai wa ikura desu ka)

_____

 ね **(ne)** _is added to the end of a sentence when the speaker would expect the listener to agree._

H For each group of words, identify the odd one out.

  1 いぬ | おとこの　ひと | にわ | ねこ

  2 くつ | はこ | そこ | かばん

  3 れいぞうこ | えき | こうえん | デパート

  4 いま | だい | まい | ひき

  5 けいたい | コンピューター | とけい | 本_{ほん}や

  6 お金_{かね} | レストラン | じかん | やくそく

Writing

I **Describe your room using the vocabulary in the box. Start with** 私のへやに (watashi no heya ni …). **Remember to mention the position of items using location words.**

Room and furniture	
いす **(isu)**	chair
ベッド **(beddo)**	bed
たんす **(tansu)**	wardrobe
ソファー **(sofā)**	sofa
テーブル **(tēburu)**	table

Japanese script

We will introduce the following five kanji in this unit.

Kanji	Reading	Meaning	Example words
男	おとこ, だん、なん (otoko/dan/nan)	*man, male*	<ruby>男<rt>おとこ</rt></ruby>の <ruby>人<rt>ひと</rt></ruby>
女	おんな、じょ (onna/jo)	*woman, female*	<ruby>女<rt>おんな</rt></ruby>の <ruby>人<rt>ひと</rt></ruby>
子	こ、し (ko/shi)	*child*	<ruby>男<rt>おとこ</rt></ruby>の <ruby>子<rt>こ</rt></ruby>、<ruby>女<rt>おんな</rt></ruby>の <ruby>子<rt>こ</rt></ruby>、<ruby>子<rt>こ</rt></ruby>ども
円	えん (en)	*yen*	1000<ruby>円<rt>えん</rt></ruby>
中	なか、ちゅう、じゅう (naka/chū/jū)	*in, inside, middle*	かばんの <ruby>中<rt>なか</rt></ruby>

J Choose the correct kanji from the box to complete the sentences.

中　　男　　子　　女　　円　　子　　本

1 こうえんに ＿＿の ＿＿＿と ＿＿の ＿＿＿が います。

2 イタリアの ネクタイは 8,000＿＿＿です。

3 かばんの ＿＿＿に ＿＿＿があります。

Self-check

Tick the box which matches your level of confidence.

    1 = very confident   2 = need more practice   3 = not confident

下のボックスにじしんがあるかないかチェックしましょう。

    1. じしんがある   2. れんしゅうがひつよう   3. じしんがない

	1	2	3
Talking about where things and people are using arimasu, imasu and location words.			
Expressing how many things/people there are using Japanese counters.			
Using Japanese numbers from 100.			
Recognizing the kanji for *man*, *woman*, *child*, *yen* and *inside*.			

* For more information talking about where things are, location words, Japanese counters and numbers from 100 refer to *Complete Japanese*, Unit 3, or *Get Started in Japanese*, Units 6 and 7.

4 ともだちと　えいがを　みました。

I saw a film with my friend.

In this unit you will learn to:

- ✅ Talk about past actions using ました (mashita).
- ✅ Use Japanese verbs for giving and receiving.
- ✅ Tell the time.
- ✅ Say what day and month it is.
- ✅ Express desires using the tai form.
- ✅ Recognize the kanji for *what*, *time*, *minute*, *eat* and *drink*.

CEFR: Can scan longer text in order to locate desired information in everyday material, such as letters, brochures and short official documents (B1); Can write a description of an event – real or imaginary (B1); Can indicate time by such phrases as *next week, last Friday, in November, 3:00* (A1).

| past
たべました
tabemashita
ate | present
たべます
tabemasu
eat | future
たべます
tabemasu
will eat |

Meaning and usage

Past tense

The past tense of the ます **(masu)** form is ました **(mashita)**. The past negative form is ませんでした **(masen deshita)**. The past tense is used as follows:

1   to describe past events and actions:

土よう日に　ともだちと　えいがを　みました。
Doyōbi ni tomodachi to eiga o mimashita.
I saw a film with my friend on Saturday.

きのう　なにも　しませんでした。
Kinō nanimo shimasen deshita.
I didn't do anything yesterday.

2   to describe completed actions, using もう **(mō** – *already/yet)*:

もう　ひるごはんを　たべましたか。
Mō hiru gohan o tabemashita ka.
Have you had lunch yet?

はい、もう　たべました。
Hai, mō tabemashita.
Yes I have (eaten).

 *To describe incomplete actions, you will need to know the て **(te)** form (see Unit 10).*

How to form the past tense

All verbs in the ます (masu) form can be turned into the past tense in the same way.

E.g. おきます (okimasu) → おきました (okimashita)

おきません (okimasen) → おきませんでした (okimasen deshita)

A Complete the table.

Present	Present negative	Past	Past negative
おきます okimasu	おきません okimasen	おきました okimashita	おきませんでした okimasen deshita
ねます nemasu		ねました nemashita	
はたらきます hatarakimasu			はたらきませんでした hatarakimasen deshita
いきます ikimasu	いきません ikimasen		
きます kimasu			きませんでした kimasen deshita
かえります kaerimasu		かえりました kaerimashita	
します shimasu	しません shimasen		
たべます tabemasu	たべません tabemasen		
のみます nomimasu		のみました nomimashita	
みます mimasu	みません mimasen		
ききます kikimasu			ききませんでした kikimasen deshita
よみます yomimasu		よみました yomimashita	
かきます kakimasu	かきません kakimasen		
べんきょうします benkyō shimasu		べんきょうしました benkyō shimashita	

けさ **(kesa)**	*this morning*
きのう **(kinō)**	*yesterday*
せんしゅう **(senshū)**	*last week*
あさ **(asa)**	*morning*
ひる **(hiru)**	*noon*
ばん **(ban)**	*evening*
かいます **(kaimasu)**	*buy*
〜に　あいます **(〜ni aimasu)**	*meet with ~*
〜と　はなします **(〜to hanashimasu)**	*talk with ~*

B **Complete the sentences by choosing the correct form of the verb.**

1 きのうの　ばん　えきで　ともだちに　_____。

  a あいます   **b** あいました   **c** あいません

2 あしたの　あさ　とうきょうへ　_____。

  a いきました   **b** いきませんでした   **c** いきます

3 せんしゅうの　月よう日に　がっこうで　ロバートさんと

_____。

  a はなしません   **b** はなします   **c** はなしました

4 私は　あまり　コーヒーを　_____。

  a のみません   **b** のみます   **c** のみました

5 けさ　なにも　_____。

  a たべました   **b** たべます   **c** たべませんでした

6 せんしゅうの　土よう日に　デパートで　けいたいを

_____。

  a かいました   **b** かいます   **c** かいません

Meaning and usage

Giving and receiving

There are three basic verbs for giving and receiving in Japanese: あげます (**agemasu**), *to give*, もらいます (**moraimasu**), *to receive* and くれます (**kuremasu**), *to give to me*. くれます (**kuremasu**) is only used when the recipient is yourself (or members of your family or social group).

1 たなかさん (**Tanaka-san**) → ロバートさん (**Robāto-san**): There are two ways of stating that Tanaka-san gave Robert something:

たなかさんは　ロバートさんに　本^{ほん}を　あげました。

Tanaka-san wa Robāto-san ni hon o agemashita.

Mr Tanaka gave a book to Robert.

> *The particle for* from *is usually* から (**kara**), *but with the verbs of giving and receiving,* あげます (**agemasu**) *and* もらいます (**moraimasu**), *the particle* に (**ni**) *is used to mean* to *and* from *respectively.*

ロバートさんは　たなかさんに　本^{ほん}を　もらいました。

Robāto-san wa Tanaka-san ni hon o moraimashita.

Robert received a book from Tanaka san.

2 私^{わたし} (**watashi**) → たなかさん (**Tanaka-san**): There is only one way of expressing *I gave something to* Tanaka-san:

私^{わたし}は　たなかさんに　本^{ほん}を　あげました。

Watashi wa Tanaka-san ni hon o agemashita.

I gave a book to Tanaka-san.

3 ロバートさん (**Robāto-san**) → 私^{わたし} (**watashi**): There are two ways of expressing that Robert gave *me* something:

私^{わたし}は　ロバートさんに　本^{ほん}を　もらいました。

Watashi wa Robāto-san ni hon o moraimashita.

I received a book from Robert.

ロバートさんは　（私^{わたし}に）　本^{ほん}を　くれました。

Robāto-san wa　(watashi ni) hon o kuremashita.

Robert gave me a book.

> *You do not usually put* 私^{わたし}に (**watashi ni**), *to me, in sentences containing* くれます (**kuremasu**) *as the recipient is usually yourself (or members of your family or social group).*

たんじょう日 (tanjōbi)	birthday
ははの日 (haha no hi)	mother's day
なんじ (nan-ji)	what time
パーティー (pātī)	party
プレゼント (purezento)	present
ケーキ (kēki)	cake
はな (hana)	flower

C **Choose the correct particles to complete the sentences. Use x if no particle is needed.**

へ、	の、	で、	に、	を、	と、	から、	まで

1 きのう _____ なんじ _____ うち _____ かえりましたか。

2 たんじょう日 _____ ロバートさん _____ プレゼント _____ もらいました。

3 木よう日 _____ 7じ _____ 9じ _____ べんきょうしました。

4 たなかさん _____ うち _____ パーティー _____ しました。

5 すずきさん _____ いっしょ _____ ケーキ _____ たべました。

6 ははの日 _____ はは _____ はな _____ あげました。

D **Choose the correct verbs to complete the sentences.**

1 たなかさんは　私に　ケーキを　（あげました／くれました）。

2 ロバートさんは　たなかさんに　本を　（くれました／もらいました）。

3 私は　すずきさんに　はなを　（くれました／あげました）。

4 やまださんは　たなかさんに　プレゼントを　（あげました／くれました）。

5 ロバートさんは　私に　とけいを　（くれました／もらいました）。

6 私は　やまださんに　フランスの　ワインを（もらいました／くれました）。

Vocabulary

Telling the time

Hour	〜じ (ji)	Minute	〜ふん (fun)/〜ぷん(pun)
1	いちじ (ichi-ji)	1	いっぷん (ippun)
2	にじ (ni-ji)	2	にふん (ni-fun)
3	さんじ (san-ji)	3	さんぷん (san-pun)
4	よじ (yo-ji)	4	よんふん (yon-fun)
5	ごじ (go-ji)	5	ごふん (go-fun)
6	ろくじ (roku-ji)	6	ろっぷん (roppun)
7	しちじ (shichi-ji)	7	ななふん (nana-fun)、しちふん (shichi-fun)
8	はちじ (hachi-ji)	8	はっぷん (happun)
9	くじ (ku-ji)	9	きゅうふん (kyū-fun)
10	じゅうじ (jū-ji)	10	じゅっぷん (juppun)
11	じゅういちじ (jūichi-ji)	15	じゅうごふん (jūgo-fun)
12	じゅうにじ (jūni-ji)	30	さんじゅっぷん (sanjuppun)、はん (han)
Question form	なんじ (nan-ji)	Question form	なんぷん

E Convert the times into Japanese.

1 *3:30* さんじさんじゅっぷん (san-ji sanjuppun) / さんじはん (san-ji han)

2 *5:12* ごじじゅうにふん (go-ji jūni-fun)

3 *12:45* _____

4 *7:18* _____

5 *9:29* _____

6 *4:02* _____

7 *8:15* _____

8 *2:50* _____

Vocabulary

Months of the year and days of the month

In Japanese, months are expressed as 'first month', 'second month' etc. The kanji for month is 月 ^{がつ}(gatsu), and the kanji for days of the month is 日 ^{にち}(nichi – but the pronunciation of this kanji varies depending on context).

Months of the year

January	いちがつ (ichi-gatsu)	1月
February	にがつ (ni-gatsu)	2月
March	さんがつ (san-gatsu)	3月
April	しがつ (shi-gatsu)	4月
May	ごがつ (go-gatsu)	5月
June	ろくがつ (roku-gatsu)	6月
July	しちがつ (shichi-gatsu)	7月
August	はちがつ (hachi-gatsu)	8月
September	くがつ (ku-gatsu)	9 月
October	じゅうがつ (jū-gatsu)	10月
November	じゅういちがつ (jūichi-gatsu)	11月
December	じゅうにがつ (jūni-gatsu)	12月
Question form	なんがつ (nan-gatsu)	なん月

Days of the month

The first ten days of the month use the counter words.

1日	ついたち (tsuitachi)	11日	じゅういちにち (jūichi-nichi)
2日	ふつか (futsuka)	12日	じゅうににち (jūni-nichi)
3日	みっか (mikka)	13日	じゅうさんにち (jūsan-nichi)
4日	よっか (yokka)	14日	じゅうよっか (jūyokka)
5日	いつか (itsuka)	15日	じゅうごにち (jūgo-nichi)
6日	むいか (muika)	16日	じゅうろくにち (jūroku-nichi)
7日	なのか (nanoka)	17日	じゅうしちにち (jūshichi-nichi)
8日	ようか (yōka)	18日	じゅうはちにち (jūhachi-nichi)
9日	ここのか (kokonoka)	19日	じゅうくにち (jūku-nichi)
10日	とおか (tōka)	20日	はつか (hatsuka)

21日	にじゅういちにち (nijūichi-nichi)	27日	にじゅうしちにち (nijūshichi-nichi)
22日	にじゅうににち (nijūni-nichi)	28日	にじゅうはちにち (nijūhachi-nichi)
23日	にじゅうさんにち (nijūsan-nichi)	29日	にじゅうくにち (nijūku-nichi)
24日	にじゅうよっか (nijūyokka)	30日	さんじゅうにち (sanjū-nichi)
25日	にじゅうごにち (nijūgo-nichi)	31日	さんじゅういちにち (sanjūichi-nichi)
26日	にじゅうろくにち (nijūroku-nichi)	Question form	なんにち (nan-nichi)

F   Convert the dates into Hiragana.

1 3月3日　　さんがつ　みっか

2 4月25日　_____

3 1月1日　_____

4 12月24日　_____

5 6月16日　_____

6 5月5日　_____

7 9月10日　_____

8 10月18日　_____

9 7月7日　_____

How to say *I want to*

The ます (masu) form can be divided into the stem and ます (masu). In かいます (kaimasu), かい (kai) is the stem. The stem plus たいです (tai desu) expresses the speaker's desire to do something.

デパートで　くつを　かいたいです。

Depāto de kutsu o kaitai desu.

I want to buy a pair of shoes at a department store.

<ruby>日本<rt>にほん</rt></ruby>へ　いきたいです。

Nihon e ikitai desu.

I want to go to Japan.

G   Using the nouns and the verbs given, make sentences that express the desire to do something.

1 ロバートさん (Robāto-san)・はなします

ロバートさんと　はなしたいです (Robāto-san to hanashitai desu)。

2 テレビ (terebi)・みます

テレビを　みたいです (Terebi o mitai desu)。

3 コーヒー (kōhī)・のみます

_____

4 うち (uchi)・かえります

_____

5 ひるごはん (hiru gohan)・たべます

_____

6 えいが (eiga)・みます

_____

7 ともだち (tomodachi)・あいます

_____

8 プレゼント (purezento)・あげます

_____

9 ケーキ (kēki)・かいます

_____

Reading

H   Read the blog written by Mr Tanaka and answer the questions in Japanese.

 PROFILE

Like • Comment • Share

7月25日（土）

きょうは、ロバートさんと　しぶやで　えいがを　みました。それから　ちかくの　レストランで　いっしょに　ばんごはんを　たべました。ロバートさんは　すしを　たべました。私は

スパゲッティーを　たべました。

あしたは　ロバートさんの　たんじょう日です。ロバートさんの　うちで　パーティーが　あります。ロバートさんに　プレゼントを　あげたいです。あした　デパートで　ネクタイを　かいます。それから　パーティーへ　いきます。

7gatsu25nichi (do)

Kyō wa Robāto san to Shibuya de eiga o mimashita. Sorekara chikaku no resutoran de issho ni ban gohan o tabemashita. Robāto-san wa sushi o tabemashita. Watashi wa supagettī o tabemashita.

Ashita wa Robāto-san no tanjōbi desu. Robāto-san no uchi de pātī ga arimasu. Robāto-san ni purezento o agetai desu. Ashita depāto de nekutai o kaimasu. Sorekara pātī e ikimasu.

1 たなかさんは　きょう　どこへ　いきましたか。

Tanaka-san wa kyō doko e ikimashita ka.

_____

2 ロバートさんと　なにを　しましたか。

Robāto-san to nani o shimashita ka.

_____

3 あしたは　なにが　ありますか。

Ashita wa nani ga arimasu ka.

_____

4 たなかさんは　あした　なにを　しますか。

Tanaka-san wa ashita nani o shimasu ka.

_____

しぶや **(Shibuya)**　　　　　　　　_Shibuya (a place in Tokyo)_

スパゲッティー **(supagettī)**　　　_spaghetti_

I **Identify the odd one out.**

1 月よう日 | 土よう日 | 水よう日 | たんじょう日

2 はな | なんじ | ケーキ | プレゼント

3 くれます | もらいます | かいます | あげます

4 せんしゅう | きのう | きょう | あした

5 あさ | ごはん | ひる | ばん

6 えき | しぶや | くつ | がっこう

 # Writing

J Describe what you did today. Make sure to include what time you got up, what time you had breakfast, lunch, etc. Also mention that you saw a film with your friend and then had dinner with him/her, then went home at 11 p.m. Use それから (sorekara) **to describe actions in sequence.**

Japanese script

We will introduce the following five kanji in this unit.

Kanji	Reading	Meaning	Example words
何	なに、なん (nani/nan)	*what*	<ruby>何<rt>なに</rt></ruby>、<ruby>何月<rt>なんがつ</rt></ruby>、<ruby>何日<rt>なんにち</rt></ruby>
時	とき、じ (toki/ji)	*time, o'clock*	<ruby>何時<rt>なんじ</rt></ruby>、10<ruby>時<rt>じ</rt></ruby>
分	わ(かる)、ふん、ぷん (wa/fun/pun)	*understand, minute, divide*	2<ruby>時<rt>じ</rt></ruby>5<ruby>分<rt>ふん</rt></ruby>、3<ruby>時<rt>じ</rt></ruby>10<ruby>分<rt>ぷん</rt></ruby>、 <ruby>分<rt>わ</rt></ruby>かります (*understand*)
食	た(べる)、しょく (ta/shoku)	*eat*	<ruby>何<rt>なに</rt></ruby>を <ruby>食<rt>た</rt></ruby>べますか
飲	の(む)、いん (no/in)	*drink*	コーヒーを <ruby>飲<rt>の</rt></ruby>みます

K **Choose the correct kanji from the box to complete the sentences.**

食	時	何時	何月何日	分	日	何	飲

1 ＿＿＿＿に　おきましたか。

2 7＿＿40＿＿です。

3 ＿を＿べますか。

4 コーヒーを＿みます。

5 たんじょう＿は＿＿＿＿＿＿＿ですか。

Self-check

Tick the box which matches your level of confidence.

1 = very confident   2 = need more practice   3 = not confident

下のボックスにじしんがあるかないかチェックしましょう。

1. じしんがある   2. れんしゅうがひつよう   3. じしんがない

	1	2	3
Talking about past actions using ました (mashita).			
Using Japanese verbs for giving and receiving.			
Telling the time.			
Saying what day and month it is.			
Expressing desires using the **tai** form.			
Recognising the kanji for *what, time, minute, eat* and *drink*.			

* For more information on using past tense, telling time, saying what day and month it is and expressing desires refer to *Complete Japanese,* Unit 4, or *Get Started in Japanese,* Units 5, 10 and 17.

5 あの　レストランは　やすいです。

That restaurant is cheap.

In this unit you will learn to:

- ✓ Use and conjugate い and な adjectives in Japanese.
- ✓ Ask questions using どう and どんな.
- ✓ Describe people, places and objects.
- ✓ Give opinions about people and things.
- ✓ Recognize the kanji for *big*, *small*, *tall*, *low* and *long*.

CEFR: Can summarize, report and give opinion about accumulated factual information on familiar matters with some confidence (B1); Can read straightforward factual texts on subjects related to his field and interest with a satisfactory level of comprehension (B1).

Meaning and usage

Adjectives are used to describe people, places and things. There are two types of adjectives in Japanese: い (**i**)-adjectives and な (**na**)-adjectives. They follow different rules when you change the tense or form.

1　い-adjectives

1.1 あの　レストランは　やすいです。 　　　 *That restaurant is **cheap**.*

1.2 あの　レストランは　やすくないです。 　　 *That restaurant is **not cheap**.*

1.3 あの　レストランは　やすくて　おいしいです。 *That restaurant is **cheap and** delicious.*

1.4 あの　レストランは　やすい　レストランです。 *That restaurant is a **cheap** restaurant.*

2　な-adjectives

2.1 たなかさんは　しんせつです。 　　　 *Mr Tanaka is **kind**.*

2.2 たなかさんは　しんせつじゃ　ないです。 　 *Mr Tanaka is **not kind**.*

2.3 たなかさんは　しんせつで　げんきです。 　 *Mr Tanaka is **kind and** healthy.*

2.4 たなかさんは　しんせつな　ひとです。 　　 *Mr Tanaka is a **kind** person.*

 2.2 can also be たなかさんは しんせつじゃ　ありません *(see Unit 1 for the basic structure of the negative form).*

Vocabulary

い -adjectives

いい	good	ながい	long
わるい	bad	みじかい	short
おおきい	big	おいしい	delicious
ちいさい	small	おもしろい	interesting, funny
たかい	high, tall, expensive	むずかしい	difficult
ひくい	low	いそがしい	busy
やすい	cheap	たのしい	enjoyable

い -adjective conjugation

The conjugation pattern for い-adjectives is regular, except for the adjective for *good* (いい). The 〜く
て form is used to connect two adjectives – see 1.3.

A   Complete the conjugation table.

Affirmative form	Negative form	Connecting two adjectives	Before nouns
いい	よくない	よくて	いい
わるい	わるくない	わるくて	わるい
おおきい			
		ちいさくて	
	たかくない		
			ひくい
やすい			
	ながくない		
		みじかくて	
			おいしい
		おもしろくて	
むずかしい			
			いそがしい
	たのしくない		

(Continued)

Vocabulary

な -adjectives

ゆうめい(な)	*famous*
にぎやか(な)	*lively*
きれい(な)	*clean, beautiful*
しずか(な)	*quiet*
しんせつ(な)	*kind*
げんき(な)	*healthy, cheerful*
ひま(な)	*free (to have free time)*
べんり(な)	*convenient*
すてき(な)	*attractive, wonderful*

 Although ゆうめい *and* きれい *end with* い *like* い*-adjectives, they are classified as* な*-adjectives.*

な -adjective conjugation

The conjugation pattern for な-adjectives is regular. The 〜で form is used to connect two adjectives – see 2.3.

B   Complete the conjugation table.

Affirmative form	Negative form	Connecting two adjectives	Before nouns
ゆうめい	ゆうめいじゃ　ない	ゆうめいで	ゆうめいな
にぎやか			
	きれいじゃ　ない		
		しずかで	
しんせつ			
			げんきな
	ひまじゃ　ない		
べんり			
		すてきで	

C   Complete the sentences by adding な only when necessary.

1 ロバートさんは　げんき＿＿＿＿＿人です。

2 この　こうえんは　しずか＿＿＿＿＿で　きれい＿＿＿＿＿です。

3 すずきさんは　すてき＿＿＿＿＿です。

4 らいしゅうの　土よう日は　ひま＿＿＿＿＿じゃないです。

5 あの　デパートは　ゆうめい＿＿＿＿＿デパートです。

6 とうきょうは　にぎやか＿＿＿＿＿ところです。

7 日本の　こうつうは　べんり＿＿＿＿＿です。

| ところ | place |
| こうつう | transport |

D   Connect the following adjectives.

1 *cheerful and interesting*

　げんきで　おもしろいです。

2 *tasty and cheap*

_____

3 *kind and attractive*

_____

4 *busy and not enjoyable*

_____

5 *quiet and beautiful*

_____

6 *lively and enjoyable*

_____

7 *long and difficult*

_____

どう and どんな

The question word for *how* is どう. It is used when asking for opinions or impressions.

Q:	あの　レストランは　どうですか。	*How is that restaurant?*
A1:	やすくて、おいしいです。	*It's cheap and delicious.*
A2:	やすいですが、おいしくないです。	*It's cheap but not delicious.*

どんな, on the other hand, is used by the speaker when they want a description or explanation. It is always followed by a noun.

 When が is attached to the end of a sentence (i.e. after です), it means but.

Q: ロバートさんは　どんな　人ですか。　　*What kind of person is Robert?*

A1: げんきな　人です。　　*He is a cheerful person.*

A2: おもしろい　人です。　　*He is an interesting person.*

E Answer the following questions using the words provided.

1 日本の　こうつうは　どうですか。(べんり・たかい)

べんりですが、たかいです。

2 あの　レストランは　どうですか。(たかい・おいしくない)

たかくて　おいしくないです。

3 日本の　たべものは　どうですか。(おいしい・たかい)

_____

4 日本の　せいかつは　どうですか。(いそがしい・たのしい)

_____

5 日本ごの　べんきょうは　どうですか。(おもしろい・たのしい)

_____

6 おしごとは　どうですか。(おもしろい・むずかしい)

_____

7 その　コンピューターは　どうですか。(やすい・いい)

_____

たべもの	food
せいかつ	life

〜は　〜が adjective です。

Many Japanese sentences containing adjectives have the form (topic) は (subject) が (adjective) です. When describing people, body parts are often marked by the subject marker が and then followed by adjectives.

ロバートさんは　<u>せ</u>が　たかいです。

Robert is tall.

*(As for Robert, (his) **back/height** is high.)*

たなかさんは　あたまが　いいです。
Mr Tanaka is clever.
*(As for Mr Tanaka, (his) **head** is good.)*

すずきさんは　めが　きれいです。
Ms Suzuki has beautiful eyes.
*(As for Ms Suzuki, (her) **eyes** are beautiful.)*

Vocabulary

Adjectives for body parts

Body part	Adjective 1	Adjective 2
せ *back, height*	せが　たかい *tall*	せが　ひくい *short*
あたま *head*	あたまが　いい *clever, intelligent*	あたまが　わるい *stupid*
め *eye*	めが　おおきい *have large eyes (large-eyed)*	めが　ちいさい *have small eyes (small-eyed)*
かみ *hair*	かみが　ながい *have long hair (long-haired)*	かみが　みじかい *have short hair (short-haired)*

F Answer the questions using the words provided.

1 ロバートさんは　どんな　人ですか。(せが　たかい・げんき)

　　せが　たかくて　げんきな　人です。

2 たなかさんは　どんな　人ですか。(あたまが　いい・しんせつ)

_____

3 すずきさんは　どんな　人ですか。(めが　おおきい・きれい)

_____

4 やまださんは　どんな　人ですか。(せが　ひくい・おもしろい)

_____

5 さとうさんは　どんな　人ですか。(かみが　みじかい・すてき)

_____

6 とうきょうは　どんな　ところですか。(にぎやか・たのしい)

_____

G **Complete the questions using the question words provided.**

どう	どんな	何 (なに)	何 (なん)	いくら	どこ	だれ

1 A: けさ、＿＿＿＿を　食(た)べましたか。

　　B: 何(なに)も　食(た)べませんでした。

2 A: あの　人(ひと)は＿＿＿＿ですか。

　　B: ロバートさんです。

3 A: おしごとは＿＿＿＿ですか。

　　B: たのしいです。

4 A: あした＿＿＿＿へ　いきますか。

　　B: とうきょうへ　いきます。

5 A: この　ワインは＿＿＿＿ですか。

　　B: 2,000円(えん)です。

6 A: きのうの　ばん、＿＿＿＿時(じ)に　うちへ　かえりましたか。

　　B: 11時(じ)に　かえりました。

7 A: すずきさんは＿＿＿＿人(ひと)ですか。

　　B: きれいな　人(ひと)です。

📖 Reading

H **Read the email from Mr Tanaka to Mr Yamada and answer the questions in Japanese.**

From:	
To:	
Subject:	

やまださん、げんきですか。私(わたし)は　げんきです。しごとは　とても
いそがしいですが、あまり　むずかしくないです。まい日(にち)　たのしいです。
かいしゃに、いい　ともだちが　います。ロバートさんと　すずきさんです。
ロバートさんは　せが　たかくて、しんせつな　人(ひと)です。すずきさんは、かみが
ながくて　すてきな　人(ひと)です。かいしゃの　ちかくの　やすくて　おいしい
レストランで　よく　いっしょに　ばんごはんを　食(た)べます。らいしゅうの
土(ど)よう日(び)、ひまですか。いっしょに　レストランへ　いきましょう。

とても　〜です	very
あまり　〜ないです	not very

1 たなかさんの　しごとは　どうですか。

_____

2 ロバートさんは　どんな　人(ひと)ですか。

_____

3 すずきさんは　どんな　人(ひと)ですか。

_____

4 かいしゃの　ちかくに　どんな　レストランが　ありますか。

_____

5 らいしゅうの　土(ど)よう日(び)に　何(なに)を　しますか。

_____

〜（だ）と　おもいます

When expressing your opinion, you can use 〜（だ）と　おもいます (_I think that_ 〜).

Before と, verbs and adjectives must be in plain forms.

い -adjective plain forms are the same as their affirmative and negative forms.

For な-adjectives, unless they are in their negative form, だ is attached at the end. だ is a plain form of です. We will deal with other plain forms in Unit 12.

日本(にほん)ごは　むずかしいと　おもいます。　　_I think Japanese is difficult._

すずきさんは　すてきだと　おもいます。　　_I think Miss Suzuki is attractive._

I　Complete the sentences by adding だ only when necessary.

1 たなかさんは　あたまが　いい_____と　おもいます。

2 日本(にほん)の　こうつうは　べんり_____と　おもいます。

3 あの　レストランは　たかくない_____と　おもいます。

4 この　しごとは　むずかしいですが、おもしろい_____と　おもいます。

5 きょうとの　こうえんは　しずかで　きれい_____と　おもいます。

6 やまださんは　しんせつ_____と　おもいます。

J **For each group of words, identify the odd one out.**

  1 おもしろい | むずかしい | おおきい | きれい

  2 ながい | ちいさい | ゆうめい | わるい

  3 いい | たのしい | ながい | おいしい

  4 しんせつ | げんき | すてき | べんり

  5 あたま | ひと | め | かみ

  6 どう | せ | どんな | だれ

Writing

K **You are expecting your parents to arrive at an airport in Japan. You cannot go to meet them as you have to work, so you want to ask your Japanese friend to pick them up. Describe your parents to your friend. Use as many adjectives as you can. Make sure you describe their appearances (such as tall, having long hair, etc.) and their personalities (cheerful, clever, etc.).**

Japanese script

We will introduce the following five kanji in this unit.

Kanji	Reading	Meaning	Example words
大	おお(きい)、だい	*big*	^{おお}大きい
小	ちい(さい)、しょう	*small*	^{ちい}小さい
高	たか(い)、こう	*high, tall, expensive*	せが ^{たか}高い
低	ひく(い)、てい	*low, short (in height)*	せが ^{ひく}低い
長	なが(い)、ちょう	*long*	かみが ^{なが}長い

L Choose the correct kanji from the box to complete the sentences.

高	大	低	長	小

1 とうきょうは ＿＿＿＿＿＿ きいです。

2 やまださんは　めが ＿＿＿＿＿＿ さいです。

3 この　ワインは ＿＿＿＿＿＿ いです。

4 たなかさんは　せが ＿＿＿＿＿＿ いです。

5 すずきさんは　かみが ＿＿＿＿＿＿ いです。

Self-check

Tick the box which matches your level of confidence.

1 = very confident   2 = need more practice   3 = not confident

下のボックスにじしんがあるかないかチェックしましょう。

1. じしんがある   2. れんしゅうがひつよう   3. じしんがない

	1	2	3
Using and conjugating い and な adjectives in Japanese.			
Asking questions using どうand どんな.			
Describing objects, people and places.			
Giving opinions about things and people.			
Recognizing the kanji for *big, small, tall, low* and *long*.			

*For more information on using and conjugating adjectives, using どう and どんな, describing objects, people and places and giving opinions refer to *Complete Japanese,* Unit 5, or *Get Started in Japanese,* Unit 11.

6

パーティーは　たのしかったです。

The party was enjoyable.

In this unit you will learn to:

- ✅ Use and conjugate adjectives in the past tense.
- ✅ Describe people, places and objects in the past.
- ✅ Give opinions about people and things in the past.
- ✅ Use で as *by means of*.
- ✅ Form adverbs from adjectives.
- ✅ Recognize the kanji for *sky*, *air*, *rain*, *electricity* and *car*.

CEFR: Can write accounts of experiences, describing feelings and reactions in simple connected text (B1); Can read straightforward factual texts on subjects related to his field and interest with a satisfactory level of comprehension (B1).

Meaning and usage

Past tense

As with the present tense, the conjugation pattern for the past tense differs for い-adjectives and な-adjectives. The conjugation pattern for な -adjectives in the past tense is also the same as for nouns.

1 い -adjectives

   1.1 パーティーは　たのしかったです。　*The party **was enjoyable**.*

   1.2 テストは　むずかしくなかったです。　*The test **was not difficult**.*

   1.3 きのうは　いそがしかったですが、おもしろかったです。*Yesterday **was busy but interesting**.*

   1.4 あの　えいがは　長くて、つまらなかったです。*That film **was long and boring**.*

2 な -adjectives

   2.1 ならは　しずかでした。　*Nara (a place in Japan) **was quiet**.*

   2.2 あの　こうえんは　きれいじゃ　なかったです。　*That park **was not clean**.*

   2.3 あの　こうえんは　にぎやかでしたが、きれいじゃ　なかったです。　*That park **was lively but not clean**.*

   2.4 ならは　しずかで、きれいでした。　*Nara **was quiet and beautiful**.*

3 nouns

   3.1 きのうは　あめでした。　*Yesterday **was rain(y)**.*
    – *It rained yesterday.*

   3.2 きのうは　いい　てんきじゃ　なかったです。
    *Yesterday **was not good weather**. – The weather was not nice yesterday.*

 ～じゃ　なかったです *can also be expressed as* ～じゃ　ありませんでした.

Vocabulary

い -adjectives

すばらしい	*wonderful*
つまらない	*boring*
おおい	*many*
人がおおい	*(there are) many people*
すくない	*few*
人がすくない	*(there are) few people*
あたたかい	*warm*
あつい	*hot*
すずしい	*cool*
さむい	*cold*

い -adjective conjugation

As with the present tense, the conjugation pattern for い -adjectives is regular except for the adjective for *good* (いい).

A   Complete the conjugation table.

Present affirmative	Past affirmative	Past negative
いいです	よかったです	よくなかったです
おいしいです	おいしかったです	おいしくなかったです
たのしいです		
すばらしいです		すばらしくなかったです
つまらないです		
おおいです	おおかったです	
すくないです		
あたたかいです		
あついです		あつくなかったです
すずしいです		
さむいです	さむかったです	

B Make sentences in the past tense using the words given.

1 パーティー・たのしい

   <u>パーティーは　たのしかったです。</u>

2 きのう・あたたかい

   _____

3 とうきょう・ひとが　おおい

   _____

4 えいが・つまらない

   _____

5 びじゅつかん・すばらしい

   _____

6 せんしゅう・さむくない

   _____

7 きのう・あつい

   _____

な -adjectives and nouns

かんたん(な)	*easy*
たいへん(な)	*hard, tough*
いや(な)	*disagreeable, unpleasant*
てんき	*weather*
あめ	*rain, rainy*
ゆき	*snow, snowy*
くもり	*cloudy*

な -adjective conjugation

The conjugation pattern for な -adjectives is regular.

C   Complete the な -adjective conjugation table.

Present affirmative	Past affirmative	Past negative
しずかです	しずかでした	しずかじゃ　なかったです
きれいです		
にぎやかです	にぎやかでした	
たいへんです		たいへんじゃ　なかったです
かんたんです		
いやです	いやでした	

D   Complete the noun conjugation table.

Present affirmative	Past affirmative	Past negative
いい　てんきです	いい　てんきでした	いい　てんきじゃ　なかったです
いやな　てんきです		
あめです	あめでした	
ゆきです		
くもりです		くもりじゃ　なかったです

E   Make sentences using the words given.

1 なら・しずか

<u>ならは　しずかでした。</u>

2 きのう・あめ

_____

3 せん月の　テスト・かんたん
       げつ

_____

4 しごと・たいへん

_____

5 せんしゅう・いやな　てんき

_____

6 おととい・くもり

_____

せん月<ruby>げつ</ruby>	*last month*
おととい	*the day before yesterday*

F   Answer the questions using the words provided.

1 しごとは　どうでしたか。(いそがしい・かんたん)

いそがしかったですが、かんたんでした。

2 しゃちょうの　スピーチは　どうでしたか。(ながい・つまらない)

_____

3 りょこうは　どうでしたか。(いい　てんき・人<ruby>ひと</ruby>が　おおい)

_____

4 えいがは　どうでしたか。(おもしろい・すばらしい)

_____

5 なつやすみは　どうでしたか。(みじかい・たのしい)

_____

6 レストランは　どうでしたか。(やすい・おいしくない)

_____

7 きょうとは　どうでしたか。(にぎやか・きれい)

_____

しゃちょう	*president of a company*
スピーチ	*speech*
りょこう	*travel*
なつ	*summer*
やすみ	*holiday, rest, day off*

The particle で

When attached to the end of place names, the particle で means *in* or *at*. When attached to objects and transport, this particle can also mean *by means of*.

きのう　くるまで　きょうとへ　いきました。	*I went to Kyoto by car yesterday.*
イギリスから　ひこうきで　きました。	*I came from England by airplane.*
じかんが　ありませんから、タクシーで　いきましょう。	*As we don't have time, let's go by taxi.*

When the particle から is attached to the end of a sentence, it means *because*.

The question word for *how, by what means* is どうやって:

| どうやって　ならへ　いきますか。 | *How do you go to Nara?* |
| タクシーで　いきます。 | *I go by taxi.* |

Vocabulary

Transport

でんしゃ	*train*
ひこうき	*airplane*
しんかんせん	*bullet train*
タクシー	*taxi*
じてんしゃ	*bicycle*
ふね	*ship*
ちかてつ	*underground, subway*
バス	*bus*

G **Complete the sentences by choosing the correct particles. If no particle is needed, use ×.**

| で | と | の | へ | から | まで |

1 しんかんせん _____ きょうと _____ いきます。

2 かんこく _____ ふね _____ きました。

3 この　くるまは　日本 _____ くるま _____ です。
（にほん）

4 あめでした _____ タクシー _____ うち _____ かえりました。

5 まいあさ _____ でんしゃ _____ かいしゃ _____ いきます。

6 うち _____ えき _____ じてんしゃ _____ いきました。

7 バス _____ ちかてつ _____ こうえん _____ いきます。

8 わたしは　ひこうき _____ イギリス _____ いきます。

 # Reading

H Read Robert's blog post and answer the questions in Japanese.

Daily Blog

せんしゅうの　土よう日に　ともだちの　たなかさんと　いっしょに
しんかんせんで　きょうとへ　いきました。きょうとえきから
タクシーで　きよみずでらへ　いきました。きよみずでらは　大きくて、
とても　ゆうめいな　おてらです。ちかくに　レストランや　みせが
たくさん　あります。とても　にぎやかで、きれいでしたが、とても
あつかったです。つぎは　ならへ　いきたいです。

1 ロバートさんは　せんしゅうの　土よう日に　どこへ　いきましたか。

_____

2 どうやって　いきましたか。

_____

3 ちかくに　何が　ありますか。

_____

4 どうでしたか。

_____

きよみずでら	Kiyomizu temple
おてら	temple
みせ	shop
たくさん	many
つぎ	next (time)

Adverbs with なります

In English, you add *ly* after adjectives to make adverbs, for example, *beautiful* → *beautifully*. In Japanese, い -adjectives and な -adjectives can be turned into adverbs in the following way:

あつい　→　あつく

きれい　→　きれいに

なります means *to become*, and often follows adverbs as well as nouns:

あつく　なります。　　　　　*It is going to become hot.*

きれいに　なりました。　　　*It has become clean.*

かいしゃいんに　なりました。 *I have become a company employee.*

In Japan, there are four seasons: はる (*spring*), なつ (*summer*), あき (*autumn*) and ふゆ (*winter*). It gets warm in spring, hot in summer, cool in autumn and cold in winter.

I Use the words to complete the paragraph. You will need to change some of the forms.

さむい	あつい	すずしい	あたたかい

日本の　はるは　3月から　5月までです。＿＿＿＿＿＿なり

ます。なつは　6月から　8月までです。＿＿＿＿＿＿なります。あ

きは　9月から　11月までです。＿＿＿＿＿＿なります。ふゆは

12月から　2月までです。日本の　ふゆは　とても＿＿＿＿＿＿です。

J For each group of words, identify the odd one out.

1 はる | なつ | ふゆ | きのう

2 あつい | おいしい | さむい | あたたかい

3 あめ | ゆき | いや | くもり

4 おおい | たいへん | つまらない | すばらしい

5 えき | じてんしゃ | タクシー | ふね

6 きょうと | せんしゅう | とうきょう | なら

 Writing

K Describe your last holiday. Try to include: where you went, who you went with, what transport you used, what you did once you were there. Describe the places you visited there. For example, were they beautiful? Were there many people there? Make sure to include how you felt about your holiday.

<table>
<tr><td></td><td></td></tr>
<tr><td></td><td></td></tr>
<tr><td></td><td></td></tr>
<tr><td></td><td></td></tr>
<tr><td></td><td></td></tr>
<tr><td></td><td></td></tr>
<tr><td></td><td></td></tr>
<tr><td></td><td></td></tr>
<tr><td></td><td></td></tr>
<tr><td></td><td></td></tr>
<tr><td></td><td></td></tr>
<tr><td></td><td></td></tr>
<tr><td></td><td></td></tr>
<tr><td></td><td></td></tr>
</table>

Japanese script

We will introduce the following five kanji in this unit.

Kanji	Reading	Meaning	Example words
天	てん	*sky, heaven*	てんき 天気
気	き	*air, spirit, mind*	き びょう気 (ill) き げん気
雨	あめ、う	*rain*	あめ 雨
電	でん	*electricity*	でんき 電気 (electricity)
車	くるま、しゃ	*car, wheel*	でんしゃ　くるま 電車、車

L **Choose the correct kanji from the box to complete the sentences.**

| 車 | 雨 | 天気 | 土 | 電車 | 気 | 私 | 日 | 高 |

1 きのうは　いい　＿＿＿＿＿＿　でした。

2 ＿＿＿＿＿よう＿＿＿＿＿は＿＿＿＿＿でした。

3 ドイツの＿＿＿＿＿は＿＿＿＿＿いです。

4 ＿＿＿の　ちちは　げん＿＿＿＿＿です。

5 まいあさ　＿＿＿＿＿＿で　かいしゃへ　いきます。

Self-check

Tick the box which matches your level of confidence.

1 = very confident   2 = need more practice   3 = not confident

下のボックスにじしんがあるかないかチェックしましょう。

1. じしんがある   2. れんしゅうがひつよう   3. じしんがない

	1	2	3
Using and conjugating adjectives in the past tense in Japanese.			
Describing objects, people and places in the past.			
Giving opinions about things and people in the past.			
Using で as *by means of.*			
Forming adverbs from adjectives.			
Recognizing the kanji for *sky, air, rain, electricity* and *car.*			

*For more information on adjectives and their use in describing past events, as well as means of transport refer to *Complete Japanese,* Unit 6, or *Get Started in Japanese,* Units 10 and 11.

7 ロバートさんは　にほんごが　わかります。

Robert understands Japanese.

In this unit you will learn to:

✅ Use the particle が to mark the object of sentences.

✅ Express ability, desire and preferences.

✅ Express *most*.

✅ Use the stem of the ます form to express the desire to do something.

✅ Use the stem of the ます form to express two actions occurring simultaneously.

✅ Use the stem of the ます form to express how to do things.

✅ Use the stem of the ます form to express going somewhere in order to do something.

✅ Recognize the kanji for *above*, *under*, *hand*, *like* and *language*.

CEFR: Can describe experiences and events, dreams, hopes and ambitions and briefly give reasons and explanations for opinions and plans (B1); Can write about everyday aspects of his environment: people, places, job (A2); Can understand texts that consist mainly of high frequency everyday or job-related language (B1).

Meaning and usage

Usually, the grammatical object of a sentence in Japanese is marked with を. For example, コーヒー in コーヒーを　飲みます. But the object of the verbs 分かります (*understand*) and あります (*have*) is marked with が instead. Some adjectives that express desire, preference and ability also require objects, and those are also marked with が.

ロバートさんは　日本ごが　分かります。 *Robert understands Japanese.*

In Japanese, when we want to say that we are proficient in a language we say we understand a language, rather than we speak it.

たなかさんは　お金が　あります。 *Mr Tanaka has money.*

私は　あたらしい　けいたいが　ほしいです。 *I want a new mobile phone.*

何が　ほしいですか。 *What would you like to have?*

ほしい is used to express the speaker's desire. It can also be used to ask what the listener wants. However, the grammatical subject of ほしい cannot be the third person. So you cannot say ロバートさんは　けいたいが　ほしいです. Also, when offering something, for example coffee, you should not say コーヒーが　ほしいですか. You should instead say コーヒーは　いかがですか or コーヒーを 飲みませんか.

私は　日本の　えいがが　すきです。	*I like Japanese films.*
私は　やさいが　きらいです。	*I dislike vegetables.*
すずきさんは　カラオケが　じょうずです。	*Ms Suzuki is good at karaoke.*
ちちは　りょうりが　へたです。	*My father is poor at cooking.*
たなかさんは　すうがくが　とくいです。	*Mr Tanaka is good at maths.*
すずきさんは　えいごが　にがてです。	*Ms Suzuki is poor at English.*

じょうず and へた refer to being *skilful* or not at some activities which require skills, such as sports, cooking, singing, drawing, etc. You should use とくい and にがて for school subjects such as mathematics and physics.

Vocabulary

分かります	*understand*
あります	*have*
すき(な)	*like, fond of*
きらい(な)	*dislike*
じょうず(な)	*good at (skill)*
へた(な)	*poor at (skill)*
とくい(な)	*good at*
にがて(な)	*poor at*
ほしい	*want*
カラオケ	*karaoke*
りょうり	*(cooked) dish, cooking*
すうがく	*maths*

A Rearrange the words to form sentences.

1 は | コンピューター | わたし | が | あたらしい | です | ほしい

_____

2 へた | ちち | りょうり | が | は | です

_____

3 です | カラオケ | が | ロバートさん | じょうず | は

_____

4 が | すずきさん | 分かりません | は | えいご

_____

5 車 | は | が | あります | たなかさん

_____

6 きらい | ビール | つま | です | は | が

_____

7 すずきさん | が | 日本りょうり | です | すき | は

_____

8 は | とくい | たなかさん | すうがく | です | が

_____

9 えいご | は | すずきさん | が | です | にがて

_____

スポーツ	sport
サッカー	football
テニス	tennis
やきゅう	baseball
おんがく	music
クラシック	classical music
ジャズ	jazz
ロック	rock
飲みもの	drinks
コーヒー	coffee
にく	meat
やさい	vegetables
さかな	fish

B Complete the following conversations.

1（スポーツ）

たなか:　　どんな　スポーツが　すきですか。

ロバート:　（サッカー）私 は　サッカーが　すきです。

すずき:　　（テニス）私 は　テニスが　すきです。たなかさんは。

たなか:　　（やきゅう）私 は　やきゅうが　すきです。

2（おんがく）

たなか:　　_____

ロバート:　（ロック）_____

すずき:　　（クラシック）_____

たなか:　　（ジャズ）_____

3（飲みもの）

たなか:　　_____

ロバート:　（ビール）_____

すずき:　　（ワイン）_____

たなか:　　（コーヒー）_____

4（食べもの）

たなか:　　_____

ロバート:　（にく）_____

すずき:　　（やさい）_____

たなか:　　（さかな）_____

〜が　いちばん　〜です。

いちばん literally means *number one*, but it can be used to denote the English equivalent of *most*. The particle で is used to mark the group or category.

日本りょうりで　何が
いちばん　おいしいですか。 *What is the most delicious among Japanese food?*

すしが　いちばん　おいしいです。 *Sushi is the most delicious.*

Notice that the particle が follows the grammatical subject in this construction. Also, when the question words (such as *what, who, when*) are the subject of a question, they are also marked by が. This is because は always marks the topic, and cannot be attached to concepts that are unknown (such as *what, who, when*).

だれ**が**　きましたか。 *Who came?*

いつ**が**　いいですか。 *When is good (for you)?*

C Complete the dialogues by choosing the correct words from the box.

> おもしろかった りょうり すき ほしい じょうず はる はは きょうと お金
> <ruby>金<rt>かね</rt></ruby>

1 A: きせつで　いつが　いちばん _____ ですか。

　 B: _____が　いちばん _____ です。

2 A: かぞくで　だれが　いちばん _____が _____ ですか。

　 B: _____が　いちばん _____が _____です。

3 A: <ruby>日本<rt>にほん</rt></ruby>で　どこが　いちばん _____ ですか。

　 B: _____が　いちばん _____ です。

4 A: いま　<ruby>何<rt>なに</rt></ruby>が　いちばん _____ ですか。

　 B: _____が　いちばん _____ です。

Time	
きせつ	season
いつ	when
いま	now

Vocabulary

Adverbs with <ruby>分<rt>わ</rt></ruby>かります

よく	well
だいたい	mostly, roughly
すこし	a little
あまり　〜ません	not very much (always with negatives)
ぜんぜん　〜ません	not at all (always with negatives)

D Create sentences using the words given.

1 ロバート・フランスご・すこし

　 ロバートさんは　フランスごが　すこし　<ruby>分<rt>わ</rt></ruby>かります。

2 エドワード・<ruby>日本<rt>にほん</rt></ruby>ご・よく

　 _____

3 すずきさん・ちゅうごくご・ぜんぜん

　 _____

4 アンさん・かたかな・だいたい

_____

5 ロバートさん・かんじ・あまり

_____

More about the ます form

In Unit 4, we saw that the stem of the ます form can be combined with たいです to express the desire to do something. Now we will look at some more uses of the ます form.

1 Combined with たいです to express desire to do something (see Unit 4):

こどもの　ころ、いしゃに　**なりたかった**です。 _I wanted to become a doctor when I was a child._

Note that when combined with たい, verbs become い -adjectives, so the past tense is formed in the same way as い -adjectives.

あした　えいがを(が)　**みたい**です。　 _I want to see a film tomorrow._

The particle を can be replaced by が. This is optional.

2 Combined with ながら to express two actions occurring simultaneously:

まいあさ、コーヒーを　**飲^のみながら、**しんぶんを　よみます。　　 _Every morning, I read the newspaper while drinking coffee._

The subject of the main verb (よみます) and the verb stem with ながら (飲みます) must be the same. In the previous sentence, the speaker is the subject of both reading the newspaper and drinking coffee.

3 Combined with かた to express how to do things:

この　かんじの　**よみかた**が　分^わかりません。　 _I don't know how to read this kanji._

かた is a noun and when combined with the stem of the ますform, it turns verbs into nouns.

4 Combined with に　いきます to express going somewhere in order to do something:

デパートへ　ネクタイを　**かいに　いきます**。　 _I am going to the department store to buy a tie._

You can also use nouns denoting activities such as かいもの (_shopping_), カラオケ, etc. before に.

E **Complete the sentences by changing the verbs in brackets into the correct form.**

1 きのうは　あつかったですから、ビールを　_____(飲^のみます)です。

2 レストランへ　ひるごはんを　_____(食^たべます)に　いきます。

3 きょうは　いそがしかったですから、何^{なに}も　_____(します)です。

4 この　かんじの　_____(かきます)が　分^わかりません。

5 ラジオを　_____(ききます)べんきょうします。

6 ロバートさんの　うちへ　_____（あそびます）に　いきました。

7 あたまが　いたいですから、うちへ　_____（かえります）です。

8 テレビを　_____（みます）ごはんを　食^たべます。

あそびます	*play, enjoy oneself*
いたい	*sore, painful*

📖 Reading

F **Read the dialogue between Robert and Ms Suzuki and answer the questions.**

	すずき:	ロバートさん、こんばん　ひまですか。
	ロバート:	はい、時^じかんが　あります。
	すずき:	カラオケを　しに　いきませんか。
	ロバート:	カラオケですか。
	すずき:	カラオケは　きらいですか。
	ロバート:	いいえ、すきですが、へたですから、あまり　しません。
	すずき:	いっしょに　いきましょう。たなかさんも　きます。
	ロバート:	そうですか。じゃあ　私^{わたし}も　いきます。

1 ロバートさんは　こんばん　ひまですか。

_____

2 すずきさんは　こんばん　何を　しますか。

_____

3 ロバートさんは　カラオケが　すきですか。

_____

4 ロバートさんは　よく　カラオケを　しますか。

_____

Vocabulary

ジャーナリスト	*journalist*
カメラマン	*photographer*
けいさつかん	*police officer*
うちゅうひこうし	*astronaut*
はいゆう	*actor*

 # Writing

G **You have decided to join an online language exchange group to practise Japanese. Post a self-introduction to this group. Make sure to include your name and nationality, as well as what you like (such as sports, music), what you would like to do (such as going to Japan), what Japanese food you like best and what you wanted to become when you were a child.**

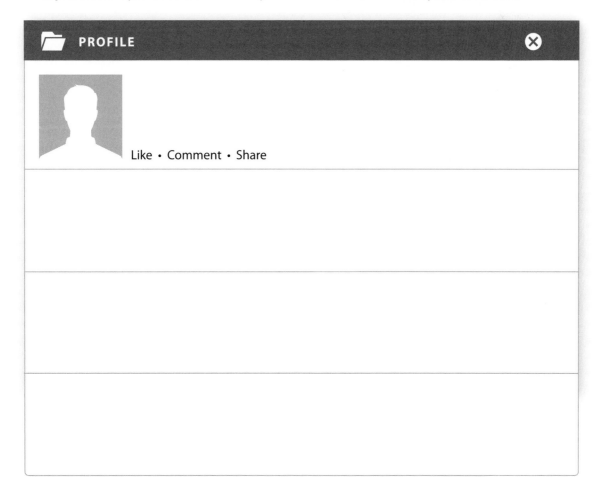

PROFILE

Like · Comment · Share

Japanese script

We will introduce the following five kanji in this unit.

Kanji	Reading	Meaning	Example words
上	うえ、あ(げます)、じょう、	*above, up*	つくえの^{うえ}上
下	した、さ(げます)、げ、か	*under, underneath*	つくえの^{した}下
手	て	*hand*	^{じょうず}上手、^{へた}下手 ^て手がみ *(letter)*
好	す(き)、こう	*like, preferable*	^す好きです
語	ご	*language*	^{にほんご}日本語, ドイツ^ご語

^{じょうず}上手 *and* ^{へた}下手 *contain unusual readings of the kanji* 下 *and* 手.

H Choose the correct kanji from the box to complete the sentences.

上	下	上手	語	日本語	好	下手

1 たなかさんは　コーヒーが　＿＿＿きです。

2 すずきさんは　えい＿＿＿が　あまり　^わ分かりません。

3 ちちは　りょうりが　＿＿＿＿＿です。

4 ロバートさんは _____が _____です。

5 木の ____に 男の 子が います。
  き   おとこ こ

6 つくえの ____に 本が あります。
                      ほん

Self-check

Tick the box which matches your level of confidence.

1 = very confident   2 = need more practice   3 = not confident

下のボックスにじしんがあるかないかチェックしましょう。

1. じしんがある   2. れんしゅうがひつよう   3. じしんがない

	1	2	3
Using the particle が to mark the object of sentences.			
Expressing ability, desire and preferences.			
Expressing *most*.			
Using the stem of the ます form to express desire to do something.			
Using the stem of the ます form to express two actions occurring simultaneously.			
Using the stem of the ます form to express how to do things.			
Using the stem of the ます form to express going somewhere in order to do something.			
Recognizing the kanji for *above, under, hand, like* and *language*.			

*For more information on describing expressing ability, desire and preferences refer to *Complete Japanese,* Unit 7, or *Get Started in Japanese,* Units 10 and 12.

8 パスポートを　みせて　ください。

Please show me your passport.

CEFR: Can write accounts of experiences, describing feelings and reactions in simple connected text (B1); Can make his opinions and reactions understood as regards solutions to problems (B1); Can give detailed instructions (B1).

Meaning and usage

The verb form that ends with て or で is called the て form, and it is used to express a variety of tenses and functions. We will look at two uses of the て form in this unit – describing sequences of actions and asking someone to do something.

1 to describe sequences of actions:

8時に　**おきて**、あさごはんを　**食べます。**　*I get up at 8 and have breakfast.*

テレビを　**みて**、ブログを　かいて、ねました。　*I watched TV, wrote a blog and went to bed.*

Note that although both sentences above use the て form, the second sentence describes a sequence of events in the past because of the tense of the last verb.

から can be added after the て form to emphasize the completion of one action before another. It is often used if the first action is a precondition of the second action.

ぎんこうへ　**いって**から、デパートへ　いきました。　*I went to a bank, and then went to a department store.*

2 to tell, request or invite others to do something:

ここに　なまえを　**かいて**　ください。　*Please write (your) name here.*

パスポートを　**みせて**　ください。　*Please show (me) your passport.*

 Remember 〜を　ください means please give me 〜. The て form followed by ください literally means please do me a favour of doing 〜.

The verb groups

In order to form the て form, you need to know about the different verb groups in Japanese. There are three verb groups – Group I, Group II and Group III (also called regular I, regular II and irregular). You can generally tell which group a verb belongs to by looking at the *sound* at the end of the ます form stem (i.e., the last sound before ます). If the stem ends in 'i' sounds, such as in のみます and かきます, then the verb belong to Group I. If it ends in 'e', as in たべます and ねます, then the verb belongs to Group II. Group III consists of the two irregular Japanese verbs: します (*do*) and きます (*come*).

Vocabulary

とめます	*stop, park*	しにます	*die*
まがります	*turn*	おしえます	*teach, tell*
つくります	*make*	えらびます	*choose*
（〜に）はいります	*enter*	やすみます	*rest*
（〜を）でます	*exit, leave*	みせます	*show*
つかいます	*use*	およぎます	*swim*
まちます	*wait*	いそぎます	*hurry*
もちます	*hold, carry*	つけます	*turn on*
でかけます	*go out*	けします	*turn off*

A Decide which group each of the verbs above belongs to.

Group I
まがります、

Group II
とめます、

There are some exceptional Group II verbs that do not follow the pattern above. You have already come across some of them. They are みます, おきます and います. There are other Group II verbs that look like Group I verbs due to the 'i' sound in the final syllable of the ます stem.

How to form the て form

Group I verbs

1 When the last sound of ます form stem is い, ち or り:

B Complete the table.

ます form	て form	English
あいます	あって	meet
	もらって	receive
つかいます		use
かいます		buy
	おもって	think

まちます	まって	wait
もちます		hold, carry

かえります	かえって	return
	分かって	understand
はいります		enter
あります		be, exist
	つくって	make
まがります		turn

2 When the last sound of ます form stem is み, び, or に:

C Complete the table.

ます form	て form	English
飲みます	飲んで	drink
	やすんで	rest
よみます		read
あそびます		play
	えらんで	choose

しにます		die

3 When the last sound of ます form stem is き or ぎ:

Note いきます belongs to this category but has an exceptional て form, いって.

D Complete the table.

ます form	て form	English
はたらきます	はたらいて	*work*
	かいて	*write*
ききます		*listen*

いきます	いって	*go*

およぎます	およいで	*swim*
いそぎます		*hurry*

4 When the last sound of ます form stem is し:

E Complete the table.

ます form	て form	English
はなします	はなして	*talk*
けします		*turn off*

Group II verbs

F Complete the table.

ます form	て form	English
ねます	ねて	*sleep*
あげます		*give*
	みせて	*show*
おしえます		*tell, teach*
	とめて	*stop, park (a vehicle)*
	食べて	*eat*
くれます		*give me*

ます form	て form	English
でかけます		*go out*
	でて	*exit*
つけます		*turn on*

ます form	て form	English
おきます	おきて	*wake up*
	いて	*be, exist*
みます		*see, watch*

Group III verbs

G Complete the table.

ます form	て form	English
します	して	*do*
べんきょうします		*study*
きます	きて	*come*

H Complete the sentences by changing the verbs in brackets.

1 ともだちに＿＿＿＿＿＿＿＿＿（あいます）、えいがを＿＿＿＿＿＿＿＿＿（みます）、うちへ　かえりました。

2 ジムへ＿＿＿＿＿＿＿＿＿（いきます）、＿＿＿＿＿＿＿＿＿（およぎます）、それから
でかけました。

3 ばんごはんを＿＿＿＿＿＿＿＿＿（つくります）、おふろに＿＿＿＿＿＿＿＿＿（はいります）、11時に
ねました。

4 8時に　うちを＿＿＿＿＿＿＿＿＿（でます）、5時まで＿＿＿＿＿＿＿＿＿（はたらきます）、それから
たなかさんと　ビールを　飲みます。

5 しんぶんを＿＿＿＿＿＿＿＿＿（よみます）、メールを＿＿＿＿＿＿＿＿＿（かきます）、スカイプで
すずきさんと＿＿＿＿＿＿＿＿＿（はなします）、テレビを　みました。

ジム	*gym*
おふろ	*bath*
スカイプ	*Skype*

I   Translate the sentences into Japanese.

1 *Please rest.*　　やすんで ください。

2 *Please show me that watch.* _____

3 *Please tell (teach) me how to read this kanji.* _____

4 *Please use this computer.* _____

5 *Please wait.* _____

6 *Please carry (hold) this bag.* _____

7 *Please choose your drink.* _____

8 *Please hurry.* _____

9 *Please turn off the TV.* _____

📖 Reading

J   Read the dialogues and answer the questions in Japanese.

たなか: すずきさん、こんばん ロバートさんの うちへ あそびに いきませんか。

すずき: いいですね。のみものを かって、私（わたし）の 車（くるま）で いきましょう。

たなか: まっすぐ いって、つぎの しんごうを みぎへ まがって ください。それから
つぎの かどを ひだりに まがって ください。ロバートさんの うちは こうえんの
まえです。

すずき: はい。

たばか: ここです。とめて ください。

たなか: ロバートさん、こんばんは。

ロバート: たなかさん、すずきさん、こんばんは。どうぞ はいって ください。

すずき: あたらしくて すてきな うちですね。

ロバート: ありがとう ございます。ピザが あります。食（た）べましょう。それから
えいがを みましょう。

1 たなかさんと　すずきさんは　どこへ　いきますか。

_____

2 どうやって　いきますか。

_____

3 ロバートさんの　うちは　どこですか。

_____

4 ロバートさんの　うちは　どんな　うちですか。

_____

5 ロバートさんの　うちで　何_{なに}を　しますか。

_____

まっすぐ	_straight_
みぎ	_right_
ひだり	_left_
しんごう	_traffic lights_
かど	_corner_
つぎ	_next_
ピザ	_pizza_

K **For each group of words, identify the odd one out.**

　1 おきます｜います｜飲_のみます｜みます

　2 はたらきます｜いきます｜ききます｜かきます

　3 かいます｜はなします｜かえります｜きます

　4 つかいます｜つくります｜あそびます｜まちます

　5 しんごう｜まっすぐ｜みぎ｜ひだり

◩ Writing

L Describe a busy weekend using the て form. Make sure to include what time you got up, had your breakfast, where you went, who you met, etc. Also make sure to describe how you felt during your weekend.

Japanese script

We will introduce the following five kanji in this unit.

Kanji	Reading	Meaning	Example words
行	い(きます), こう	*go*	行^いきます ぎん行^{こう} (bank)
来	き(ます), らい	*come*	来^きます 来月^{らいげつ} (next month)
見	み(ます), けん	*see, watch*	見^みます
右	みぎ, ゆう	*right*	右^{みぎ}
左	ひだり, さ	*left*	左^{ひだり}

M Choose the correct kanji from the box to complete the sentences.

行　　　来　　　左　　　見　　　右　　　行　　　来

1 ＿＿＿月、日本へ　＿＿＿＿＿きます。

2 たなかさんと　すずきさんが　私^{わたし}の　うちへ　＿＿＿＿＿ました。

3 ぎん＿＿＿＿の　＿＿＿＿＿に　本^{ほん}やが　あります。

4 つぎの　しんごうを　＿＿＿＿＿へ　まがって　ください。

5 へやで　ビールを　飲^のみながら　テレビを　＿＿＿＿＿ます。

Self-check

Tick the box which matches your level of confidence.

1 = very confident   2 = need more practice   3 = not confident

下のボックスにじしんがあるかないかチェックしましょう。

1. じしんがある   2. れんしゅうがひつよう   3. じしんがない

	1	2	3
Identifying each Japanese verb group.			
Forming the て form.			
Expressing sequences of actions.			
Expressing requests.			
Giving and understanding directions.			
Recognizing the kanji for *go, come, see, right* and *left*.			

*For more information on verb groups and the て form refer to *Complete Japanese,* Unit 8.

9 ここで　たべても　いいです。

You may eat here.

In this unit you will learn to:

✅ Form the て form.

✅ Ask for and grant permission.

✅ Express prohibition.

✅ Recognize verbs that require the particle に after place names.

✅ Recognize the kanji for *enter, exit, talk* and *rest*.

CEFR: Can invite others to give their views on how to proceed (B1); Can write very brief reports to a standard, conventionalized format, which pass on routine factual information and state reasons for actions (B1); Can briefly give reasons and explanations for opinions and plans, and actions (B1).

Meaning and usage

In this unit we will practise how to ask for and grant permission, and how to express prohibition, using the て form.

1 to ask for and grant permission: て form ＋も　いいです:

　　ここで　食べても　いいです。　*You may eat here.*

　　ここで　けいたいを　つかっても　いいです。　*You may use mobile phone(s) here.*

　　ここで　食べても　いいですか。　*May I eat here?*

　　ここで　けいたいを　つかっても　いいですか。　*May I use mobile phone(s) here?*

The structure て form ＋も is in fact a conditional form, meaning *even if*. So ここで　けいたいを　つかっても　いいですか literally means *Is it OK even if I use my mobile here?*

If you want to grant permission, you can simply say はい、いいですよ. If you do not want to grant permission, but do not want to sound abrupt, you may say すみません、ちょっと. ちょっと means *little* and it is an euphemistic way of expressing you will be inconvenienced a little.

In conversations, よ is added to the end of a sentence to give more assertion. ね (Unit 3), on the other hand, is added to the end of a sentence when the speaker would expect the listener to agree.

2 to express prohibition: て form + は　いけません.

ここで　食べては　いけません。　*You must not eat here.*

ここで　けいたいを　つかっては　いけません。　*You must not use the mobile phone here.*

いけません means *not allowed* or *no good*. A less formal term, ダメです may be used in place of いけません between friends and families.

 Remember that は *here is pronounced 'wa' as it is the topic marker.*

Vocabulary

おきます　I	*put*
たちます　I	*stand up*
すわります　I	*sit down*
(まどを)　あけます　II	*open (the window)*
(まどを)　しめます　II	*close (the window)*
(しゃしんを)　とります　I	*take (the picture)*
(たばこを)　すいます　I	*smoke (the cigarette)*
かります　II	*borrow*
かします　I	*lend*
うんてんします　III	*drive*
おさけ	*alcohol, sake*

 おさけ *is the politer term for* **さけ** *(alcohol, sake).*

A **Complete the tables.**

Group I

ます **Form**	て **Form**
おきます	
	たって
すわります	
	とって
	すって
かします	

Group II

ます Form	て Form
あけます	
	しめて
かります	

Group III

ます Form	て Form
うんてんします	

B **Complete the sentences by changing the verbs in brackets into the correct form.**

1 あついですね。まどを _____ (あけます)も　いいですか。

2 ここに _____ (すわります)も　いいですか。

3 5時に _____ (かえります)も　いいですか。

4 さむいですね。まどを _____ (しめます)も　いいですか。

5 ここに　かばんを _____ (おきます)も　いいですか。

6 この本を _____ (かります)も　いいですか。

C **Complete the sentences by changing the verbs in brackets into the correct form.**

1 ここで　たばこを _____ (すいます) は　いけません。

2 こうえんの　中に　車を _____ (とめます)は　いけません。

3 ここに _____ (はいります)は　いけません。

4 びじゅつかんで　しゃしんを_____(とります)は　いけません。

5 おさけを _____ (飲みます), 車を _____ (うんてんします) は　いけません。

The particles で and に

As seen in the Exercise B2 and 5, and C2 and 3, verbs such as *sit down*, *put*, *enter* and *park (a vehicle)* trigger the particle に, rather than で, after place names. Remember that the particle で is attached after place names to express some *actions* taking place in or at the place in question.

D **Complete the sentences by choosing either で or に.**

1 ここ(で／に)かばんを　おきます。

2 たなかさんの　うち(で／に)ビールを　飲みます。

3 へや(で／に)はいります。

4 いす(で／に)すわります。

5 レストラン(で／に)ばんごはんを　食べます。

6 ぎん行の　まえ(で／に)車を　とめます。

7 かいしゃ(で／に)はたらきます。

E **Complete the sentences by changing the verbs in brackets into the appropriate form.**

1 日本へ　日本語を ＿＿＿＿＿ (べんきょうします)に ＿＿＿＿＿ (行きます) たいです。

2 みなさん、＿＿＿＿＿ (たちます)ください。

3 しらない　人に　お金を ＿＿＿＿＿ (かします)は　いけません。

4 おさけを ＿＿＿＿＿ (飲みます)、＿＿＿＿＿ (およぎます)は　いけません。

5 この　かんじの ＿＿＿＿＿ (よみます)かたが　分かりません。＿＿＿＿＿ (おしえます)ください。

6 けいたいを ＿＿＿＿＿ (つかいます)ながら、車を ＿＿＿＿＿ (うんてんします) は　いけません。

7 ビールを ＿＿＿＿＿ (飲みます)ながら、テレビを ＿＿＿＿＿ (見ます)たいです。

8 金よう日ですから、はやく＿＿＿＿＿ (かえります)も　いいです。

みなさん	*everyone*
しらない　人	*stranger (person you don't know)*
はやく	*early*

F **Robert is visiting his local library for the first time. Choose the correct sentence to complete each gap in the conversation.**

1 コーヒーを　飲んでも　いいですか。

2 ラップトップを　つかっても　いいですか。

3 はい、そうです。

4 はい、分かりました。

ロバート:　　　　　こんにちは。

女の人:　　　　　こんにちは。きょう、はじめてですか。

ロバート:　　　　　＿＿＿＿＿＿＿＿＿＿＿＿＿＿＿＿

女の人:　　　　　それでは、ルールを　せつめいします。ここで　食べものを　食べては　いけません。

ロバート:　　　　　＿＿＿＿＿＿＿＿＿＿＿＿＿＿＿＿

女の人:　　　　　いいえ、飲みものも　飲んでは　いけません。たばこも　すっては　いけません。

ロバート:　　　　　　_____

女の人（おんな ひと）:　それから、けいたいを　つかっては　いけません。ともだちと　話（はな）しては
いけません。

ロバート:　　　　　　_____

女の人（おんな ひと）:　はい、ラップトップは　つかっても　いいですが、ヘッドホンを　つかって
ください。本（ほん）は　3さつまで　かりても　いいです。ここに　なまえを　かいて
ください。

はじめて	*for the first time*
ルール	*rules*
せつめいします　III	*explain*
ラップトップ	*laptop*
ヘッドホン	*headphone*
～さつ	*counter for books and magazines*

📖 Reading

G　Read Robert's blog and answer the questions in Japanese.

日本（にほん）では、20さいまで　おさけを　飲（の）んでは　いけません。たばこも
20さいまで　すっては　いけません。イギリスでは、パブや
レストランで　たばこを　すっては　いけませんが、日本（にほん）では、
きつえんせきで　すっても　いいです。

車（くるま）は　18さいから　うんてんしても　いいです。オートバイは
16さいからです。男（おとこ）の　人（ひと）は　18さいから　けっこんしても　いいです。
女（おんな）の　人（ひと）は　16さいまで　けっこんしては　いけません。

1 日本では、何さいから　おさけを　飲んでも　いいですか。

_____

2 日本の　レストランで　たばこを　すっても　いいですか。

_____

3 日本では、何さいから　車を　うんてんしても　いいですか。

_____

4 日本では、女の　人は　何さいから　けっこんしても　いいですか。

_____

～さい	_years old_
パブ	_pub_
きつえんせき	_smoking area_
オートバイ	_motorcycles_
けっこんします　III	_get married_

 You have probably noticed the topic marker は follows 日本で and イギリスで in the text. This is because what happens in Japan and Britain is the topic of this text. It also highlights a contrast – that this happens in Japan/Britain instead of elsewhere.

Vocabulary

H What are the opposites of these words?

1 おもしろい　<u>つまらない</u>

2 みぎ　_____

3 あつい　_____

4 大きい　_____

5 高い　_____

6 つけます　_____

7 おきます　_____

8 かします　_____

9 あけます　_____

10 たちます　_____

I For each group of words, identify the odd one out.

1 すわります | およぎます | はいります | とめます

2 おさけ | ワイン | コーヒー | ビール

3 あけます | しめます | かります | かします

4 まど | いす | テーブル | ベッド

5 うんてんします | べんきょうします | 話します | せつめいします

6 とります | すいます | かえります | かります

✏ Writing

J **Describe to your Japanese friends what you are allowed or not allowed to do in your country.**
For example, from what age can you drink alcohol or smoke a cigarette? For example,
イギリスでは、18さいまで　おさけを　飲んでは　いけません。たばこは…

Japanese script

We will introduce four kanji in this unit.

Kanji	Reading	Meaning	Example words
入	はい(ります), にゅう	*enter, go in*	へやに　入ります
出	で(ます), しゅつ	*exit, go out*	へやを　出ます
話	はな(します), はなし, わ	*talk, story*	ともだちと　話します
休	やす(みます), やす(み),　きゅう	*rest, days off*	がっこうを　休みます

K　Choose the correct kanji to complete the sentences.

| 土 | 右 | 休 | 入 | 出 | 行 | 来 | 話 | 日 |

1　＿＿＿＿＿＿ しゅう、レストランへ ＿＿＿＿＿＿ きます。

2　レストランの ＿＿＿＿＿＿ に　こうえんが　あります。

3　＿＿＿＿＿＿ よう ＿＿＿＿＿＿ は　うちで ＿＿＿＿＿＿ みます。

4　きのう　ロバートさんと　日本語で ＿＿＿＿＿＿ しました。

5　まいあさ　8時はんに　うちを ＿＿＿＿＿＿ ます。

6　この　へやに ＿＿＿＿＿＿ っても　いいですか。

Self-check

Tick the box which matches your level of confidence.

1 = very confident　　　2 = need more practice　　　3 = not confident

下のボックスにじしんがあるかないかチェックしましょう。

1. じしんがある　　　2. れんしゅうがひつよう　　　3. じしんがない

	1	2	3
Forming the て form.			
Asking for and granting permission.			
Expressing prohibition.			
Recognizing verbs that require the particle に after place names.			
Recognizing the kanji for *enter, exit, talk* and *rest*.			

*For more information on expressing permission and prohibition using the て form refer to *Complete Japanese*, Unit 8.

10 いま　ばんごはんを　たべて　います。

I am eating dinner now.

In this unit you will learn to:

✔ Form the continuous/progressive tense.

✔ Express what is happening at the time of speaking or at a certain time in the past.

✔ Describe actions that are in process even if you are not actually doing it at the time of speaking.

✔ Describe habitual actions that take place regularly.

✔ Describe a continuous state which happened in the past.

✔ Describe things you haven't done yet or are still in process of doing.

✔ Use the particle で.

✔ Recognize the kanji for *now, study, school* and *live.*

CEFR: Can read straightforward factual texts on subjects related to his field and interest with a satisfactory level of comprehension (B1); Can write a description of an event – real or imaginary (B1); Can describe experiences and events, dreams, hopes and ambitions and briefly give reasons and explanations for opinions and plans (B1).

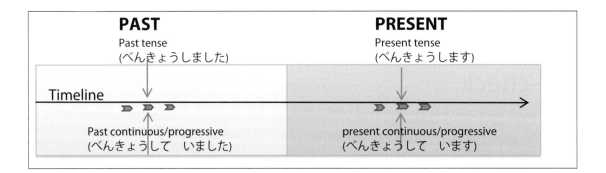

Meaning and usage

The present continuous/progressive tense (expressed in English by the ending *ing*) is expressed in Japanese by using the て form plus います. The negative form is the て form plus いません, while the past affirmative and negative forms are て form plus いました and て form plus いませんでした respectively.

	Affirmative	**Negative**
Present	て form plus います	て form plus いません
Past	て form plus いました	て form plus いませんでした

The continuous/progressive tense is used as follows:

1 to describe actions taking place at the time of speaking (present continuous/progressive), or at certain points in the past (past continuous/progressive). When describing actions taken at the time of speaking, いま (*now*) is often used with the continuous/progressive tense:

ロバートさんは　いま　何_{なに}を　して　いますか。　*What are you doing now, Robert?*

いま　ばんごはんを　食_たべて　います。　*I am eating dinner now.*

いま　何_{なに}も　して　いません。　*I am not doing anything at the moment.*

きのうの　ばん　何_{なに}を　して　いましたか。　*What were you doing last night?*

ともだちと　えいがを　見_みて　いました。　*I was watching a movie with my friend.*

2 to describe actions that are in progress, even if you are not actually doing it at the time of speaking:

いま　とても　おもしろい　本_{ほん}を　よんで　います。　*I am (currently) reading a very interesting book.*

3 to describe habitual actions that take place regularly:

火ようび日の　ばん、日本語_{にほんご}の　がっこうで　日本語_{にほんご}を　べんきょうして　います。
I study Japanese at a Japanese language school on Tuesday evenings.

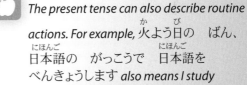

The present tense can also describe routine actions. For example, 火_かよう日_びの　ばん、日本語_{にほんご}の　がっこうで　日本語_{にほんご}を　べんきょうします *also means I study Japanese at a Japanese language school on Tuesdays. Using the progressive tense emphasizes that you are in the habit of doing the action.*

4 to describe a continuous state where the initial event happened in the past, such as being married. Verbs such as *live* and *know* belong to this group:

たなかさんは　けっこんして　います。
Mr Tanaka is married.

たなかさんは　ロバートさんを　よく　しって　います。
Mr Tanaka knows Robert well.

The negative form of しって います, *the verb to know, is always* しりません.

5 to describe things you haven't done yet or are still in process of doing using まだ:

もう　ごはんを　食_たべましたか。　*Have you eaten already?*

いいえ、まだ　食_たべて　いません。　*No, I haven't eaten yet.*

もう　その　本_{ほん}を　よみましたか。　*Have you read that book yet?*

いいえ、まだ　よんで　います。　*No, I am still reading it.*

もう means *already* while まだ means *yet* with negative continuous/progressive forms, or *still* with affirmative continuous/progressive forms.

 To express that you have already eaten, you simply use the past tense using もう: はい、もう 食_たべました.

Vocabulary

(雨_{あめ}が)　ふります　Ⅰ	*rain (rain falls)*
(電話_{でんわ}を)　かけます　Ⅱ	*make (a phone call)*
ならいます　Ⅰ	*learn*
うります　Ⅰ	*sell*
しります　Ⅰ	*know*
すみます　Ⅰ	*live*
きます　Ⅱ	*wear (clothes)*
(〜に)　れんらくします　Ⅲ	*contact*
しんせん(な)	*fresh*
ギター	*guitar*
はし	*chopsticks*
コンピューターソフト	*software*
しょうせつ	*novel*
大_{だい}がく	*university*
レポート	*report*
ジュース	*juice*
さいきん	*recently*
何_{なに}か	*something*
もう	*already, yet*
まだ	*yet, still*
いま	*now*

A Complete the tables.

Group I

ます Form	て Form
ふります	
	ならって
うります	
しります	
	すんで

Group II

ます Form	て Form
	かけて
きます	

Group III

ます Form	て Form
れんらくします	

B Translate the sentences into Japanese.

1 *I am eating breakfast now.*　いま　あさごはんを　食べて　います。

2 *It's raining now.* _____

3 *Robert is making a phone call now.* _____

4 *I am listening to (some) music now.* _____

5 *I am resting now.* _____

6 *Robert was talking with Mr Tanaka.* _____

7 *Miss Suzuki was reading a newspaper.* _____

C Complete the sentences by changing the verbs in brackets into the correct form.

1 さいきん　何か _____ (します)か。

2 いま　ギターを _____ (ならいます)。

3 いま　おもしろい　DVDを _____ (かります)。

4 いま　しょうせつを _____ (かきます)。

5 いま　あたらしい　コンピューターソフトを _____ (つくります)。

D Rearrange the words to create sentences.

1 やすい|どこ|を|うって　います|で|コンピューター|か

_____

2 はたらいて　います|9時(じ)|まい日(にち)|まで|から|5時(じ)

_____

3 えい語(ご)|がっこう|えい語(ご)|の|で|を|べんきょうして　います

_____

4 すずきさん|はたらいて　います|で|ぎん行(こう)|は

_____

5 ジュース|やさい|で|しんせんな|つくって　います|を|まいあさ

_____

6 日本語(にほんご)|で|おしえて　います|私(わたし)|は|を|大(だい)がく

_____

7 あの|何(なに)|うって　います|を|か|みせ|で

_____

8 かぞく|の|くに|に|で|れんらくして　います|メイル|いつも

_____

📖 Reading

E James and Mr Tanaka are at a party. Read the conversation and answer the questions in Japanese.

たなか:　　はじめまして、たなかです。

ジェームス:　はじめまして、ジェームスです。

たなか:　　ジェームスさんの　おくには　どちらですか。

ジェームス:　私(わたし)は　イギリスから　来(き)ました。

たなか:　　そうですか。ロバートさんを　しって　いますか。

ジェームス:　いいえ、しりません。

たなか:　　あの　せが　高(たか)い　人(ひと)です。スーツを　きて　います。ロバートさんも
　　　　　　イギリス人(じん)です。

ジェームス:　たなかさんは　けっこんして　いますか。

たなか: 　はい、けっこんして　います。子どもが　ふたり　います。ジェームスさんは?

ジェームス: 私は　けっこんして　いません。たなかさんは　どこに　すんで　いますか。

たなか: 　あさくさに　すんで　います。ジェームスさんは?

ジェームス: 私は　しんじゅくに　すんで　います。

たなか: 　休みの　日に　何を　して　いますか。

ジェームス: 私は　ドライブが　好きですが、車を　もって　いませんから、たいてい　うちで
　　　　　　えいがを　見て　います。

たなか: 　そうですか。来しゅうの　土よう日、ロバートさんと　よこはまへ
　　　　　車で　あそびに　行きます。ジェームスさんも　来ませんか。

ジェームス: はい、行きたいです。

1　ジェームスさんは　ロバートさんを　しって　いますか。

_____

2　ジェームスさんは　けっこんして　いますか。

_____

3　ジェームスさんは　どこに　すんで　いますか。

_____

4　ジェームスさんは　休みの　日に　何を　して　いますか。

_____

5　ジェームスさんは　来しゅうの　土よう日に　何を　しますか。

_____

スーツ	suits
あさくさ	Asakusa (a place in Tokyo)
しんじゅく	Shinjuku (a place in Tokyo)
よこはま	Yokohama (a city near Tokyo)

Verbs of motion in the continuous/ progressive tense

When verbs of motion, such as 行きます, 来ます, かえります or 出かけます, are in the continuous/ progressive form, it can be difficult to tell whether they are expressing a habitual action or a continuous state (see points 3 and 4 in Meaning and usage). The clue often lies in contexts – if a sentence contains phrases such as *every week, every morning,* etc., then it expresses a habitual action. If, on the other hand, the word *now* is used, then it expresses a continuous state:

ロバートさんは　まいしゅう　火よう日に、日本語の　がっこうへ
行って　います。

Robert goes to a Japanese school every Tuesday – habitual action

ロバートさんは　いま、がっこうへ　行って　います。

Robert has gone to the school and still there – continuous state

F **Decide whether the statements have either the meaning of A (habitual actions) or B (continuous states).**

1 ロバートさんは　いま　しんじゅくへ　行って　います。(B)

2 つまは　まいしゅう　土よう日に　ともだちと　出かけて　います。(A)

3 いま　ともだちが　あそびに　来て　います。(　)

4 ロバートさんは　いま　イギリスへ　かえって　います。(　)

5 ちちは　いま　ちょっと　出かけて　います。(　)

6 すずきさんは　まいしゅう　水よう日に　テニスクラブへ　行って　います。(　)

7 たなかさんは　まいあさ　8時はんに　かいしゃへ　来て　います。(　)

G **Complete the sentences by choosing the correct form.**

1 A: もう　レポートを＿＿＿＿＿＿＿か。

   a かきます　　　　**b** かきました　　　　**c** かいて　いません

  B: いいえ、まだ＿＿＿＿＿＿＿。コーヒーを　飲んでから　かきます。

   a かきます　　　　**b** かきました　　　　**c** かいて　いません

2 A: もう　ひるごはんを＿＿＿＿＿＿＿か。

   a 食べます　　　　**b** 食べました　　　　**c** 食べて　いません

  B: いいえ、まだ＿＿＿＿＿＿＿。

   a 食べます　　　　**b** 食べました　　　　**c** 食べて　いません

A: じゃ、いっしょに　レストランへ　_____に　行きましょう。

    a 食べ   **b** 食べました   **c** 食べて

3 A: まだ　メイルを　_____か。

    a よみます   **b** よみません   **c** よんで　います

B: いいえ、もう　_____。

    a よみます   **b** よみました   **c** よんで　います

The particle で

So far, we have seen five uses of the particle で.

1 It indicates an action taking place at or in somewhere.

こうえんで　サッカーを　します。　*I play football in a park.*

2 It indicates a mode of transport.

電車で　かいしゃへ　行きます。　*I go to work by train.*

3 It indicates a category.

日本りょうりで　すしが　いちばん　好きです。　*Out of all Japanese food I like sushi the most.*

4 It indicates a language that you are saying or doing something in.

ロバートさんと　日本語で　話します。　*I talk with Robert in Japanese.*

5 It indicates a method used for actions.

いつも　メイルで　かぞくに　れんらくします。　*I contact my family via email.*

H Decide which meaning the particle で has and match the correct number from the examples above.

1 レストランで　ひるごはんを　食べます。(1)

2 かいしゃで　9時から　5時まで　はたらきます。( )

3 えい語で　メイルを　かきます。( )

4 はしで　ごはんを　食べます。( )

5 雨が　ふって　いますから、タクシーで　行きましょう。( )

6 しんせんな　やさいで　ジュースを　つくります。( )

7 スポーツで　やきゅうが　いちばん　好きです。( )

 # Writing

J You are going to a party. You are going to meet new people, so write some notes to introduce yourself. Make sure to include where you live, if you are married or not, etc. Also make sure you mention what you habitually do on weekends, for example what your hobbies are.

Japanese script

We will introduce four kanji in this unit.

Kanji	Reading	Meaning	Example words
今	いま、こん	now, current	<ruby>今<rt>いま</rt></ruby> <ruby>食<rt>た</rt></ruby>べています <ruby>今<rt>こん</rt></ruby>しゅう (this week) <ruby>今月<rt>こんげつ</rt></ruby> (this month) <ruby>今日<rt>きょう</rt></ruby>
学	まな(ぶ)、がく、がっ	study	<ruby>大学<rt>だいがく</rt></ruby>
校	こう	school	<ruby>学校<rt>がっこう</rt></ruby> <ruby>小学校<rt>しょうがっこう</rt></ruby> (elementary school) <ruby>中学校<rt>ちゅうがっこう</rt></ruby> (junior high school) <ruby>高校<rt>こうこう</rt></ruby> (high school)
生	い(きる)、う(まれる)、せい	live	<ruby>学生<rt>がくせい</rt></ruby> <ruby>小学生<rt>しょうがくせい</rt></ruby> <ruby>中学生<rt>ちゅうがくせい</rt></ruby> <ruby>高校生<rt>こうこうせい</rt></ruby> <ruby>大学生<rt>だいがくせい</rt></ruby>

K Choose the correct kanji to complete the sentences.

| 出 | 入 | 見 | 食 | 今 | 学生 | 休 | 話 | 今 | 今日 | 学校 |

1 すずきさんは _____ おふろに _____ っています。

2 _____ で、ともだちと _____ します。

3 テレビを _____ て、ごはんを _____ べて、ねます。

4 _____ は _____ かけません。_____ みます。

5 <ruby>私<rt>わたし</rt></ruby>は _____ です。

6 _____ しゅうから　たばこを　すいません。

Self-check

Tick the box which matches your level of confidence.

1 = very confident   2 = need more practice   3 = not confident

下のボックスにじしんがあるかないかチェックしましょう。

1. じしんがある   2. れんしゅうがひつよう   3. じしんがない

	1	2	3
Forming the continuous/progressive tense.			
Expressing what is happening at the time of speaking or at a certain time in the past.			
Describing actions that are in process even if you are not actually doing it at the time of speaking.			
Describing habitual actions that take place regularly.			
Describing a continuous state which happened in the past.			
Describing things you haven't done yet or are still in process of doing.			
Using the particle で.			
Recognizing the kanji for *now*, *study*, *school* and *live*.			

*For more information on continuous/progressive tense using the て form refer to *Complete Japanese*, Unit 9.

11 にほんへ いって みたいです。

I would like to go to Japan.

In this unit you will learn to:

- ✅ Express trying to do something (for the first time).
- ✅ Express completion of actions, often with regret.
- ✅ Express good will and gratitude.
- ✅ Identify clothing terms.
- ✅ Use the particle に.
- ✅ Recognize the kanji for *precedence*, *father*, *mother* and *white*.

CEFR: Can describe experiences and events, dreams, hopes and ambitions and briefly give reasons and explanations for opinions and plans (B1); Can write accounts of experiences, describing feelings and reactions in simple connected text (B1).

Meaning and usage

The て form can be combined with other verbs to express trying to do something for the first time, the completion of actions and to express good will/gratitude.

1   to express trying to do something (for the first time) using て form + みます:

せんしゅう、はじめて　すしを　食べて　みました。
I tried sushi for the first time last week.
日本へ　行って　みたいです。
I would love to go to Japan. (I have never been there before.)

この　スーツを　きて　みても　いいですか。
May I try this suit on?

2   to express completion of actions using て form + しまいます:
きのうの　ばん、テレビを　見ながら　ねて　しまいました。
I fell asleep while watching TV.

しまいます means *finish* doing something and is rarely used on its own. Depending on the context, this form is also used to convey regret or embarrassment for having done something. For example, the above sentence can convey regret or embarrassment if the speaker intended to do something else but fell asleep and couldn't.

3   to express good will and gratitude using て form + あげます/もらいます/くれます:

あげます/もらいます/くれます are used when we give and receive gifts. But we often give and receive *actions*. It is very important in Japanese to linguistically acknowledge good will and gratitude by using this form.

たなかさんは　ロバートさんに　お金<ruby>を<rt>かね</rt></ruby>　かして　あげました。

Mr Tanaka (kindly) lent some money to Robert. (Mr Tanaka is the giver of the action of lending some money to Robert.)

私<ruby>は<rt>わたし</rt></ruby>　ロバートさんに　お金<ruby>を<rt>かね</rt></ruby>　かして　もらいました。

I borrowed some money from Robert.

It is difficult to give a literal translation for this form. Here, I am the receiver of Robert's kind action of lending me some money.

ロバートさんは　(私<ruby>に<rt>わたし</rt></ruby>)　お金<ruby>を<rt>かね</rt></ruby>　かして　くれました。

Robert (kindly) lent (me) some money.

Vocabulary

つれて　行<ruby>きます<rt>い</rt></ruby>　I	*take (someone)*
(人<ruby>を<rt>ひと</rt></ruby>)　おくります　I	*escort (someone)*
しょうかいします　III	*introduce*
あんないします　III	*show around*
てつだいます　I	*help, lend a hand*
はきます　I	*put on (shoes, trousers, etc.)*
かぶります　I	*put on (a hat, etc.)*
かんがえます　II	*think*
わすれます　II	*forget*
やります　I	*do*
まちがえます　II	*make a mistake*
なくします　I	*lose*
おとします　I	*drop, lose*
しろい	*white*
もう　いちど	*one more time*
ぜんぶ	*all*
みち	*road, way*
かぎ	*key*
さいふ	*wallet*
パスポート	*passport*
コート	*coat*
ぼうし	*hat*

いみ	*meaning*
月<ruby>つき</ruby>	*moon*
せんせい	*teacher (when addressing one's teacher)*

A Rearrange the words to form sentences.

1 みたい | へ | 月<ruby>つき</ruby> | です | 行<ruby>い</ruby>って

_____

2 くつ | を | も | いいです | みて | はいて | この | か

_____

3 みます | もう　いちど | かんがえて

_____

4 みて | あの | きて | も | コート | いいです | か | しろい | を

_____

5 すし | はじめて | みました | を | きのう | 食<ruby>た</ruby>べて

_____

6 ぼうし | です | みたい | その | を | かぶって

_____

B Translate the sentences into Japanese using the verbs in brackets.

1 *I (regretfully) lost my keys.* (なくします)

　かぎを　なくして　しまいました。

2 *I (regretfully) forgot (to bring) the passport.* (わすれます)

_____

3 *I (regretfully) dropped (lost) my wallet.* (おとします)

_____

4 *I will finish this job.* (やります)

_____

5 *I (regretfully) lost the way.* (まちがえます)

_____

6 *I will finish writing this report tonight.* (かきます)

_____

7 *I have eaten all the cake.* (たべます)

_____

C **Create sentences expressing what 'I' have done for Robert using the given words.**

1 みち・おしえます
　私は　ロバートさんに　みちを　おしえて　あげました。

_____

2 本・かします

_____

3 ケーキ・つくります

_____

4 かんじの　いみ・せつめいします

_____

5 ジェームスさん・しょうかいします

_____

6 りょこうの　しゃしん・見せます

_____

D **Choose the correct verbs to complete the sentences.**

1 私は　やまだせんせいに　日本語を　_____　もらいました。
　　a ならって　　　　　　**b** べんきょうして　　**c** おしえて

2 私は　たなかさんに　きょうとを　_____　もらいました。
　　a しょうかいして　　　**b** あんないして　　　**c** せつめいして

3 ロバートさんは　たなかさんに　お金を　_____　もらいました。
　　a かして　　　　　　　**b** あげて　　　　　　**c** かりて

4 ロバートさんは　すずきさんに　きょうとへ　_____　もらいました。
　　a かえって　　　　　　**b** つれて　行って　　　**c** あんないして

5 私は　たなかさんに　しごとを　_____　もらいました。
　　a てつだって　　　　　**b** つかって　　　　　**c** かして

6 私は　やまだせんせいに　えきまで　_____　もらいました。
　　a おくって　　　　　　**b** せつめいして　　　**c** しょうかいして

E **Paraphrase the sentences using 〜て くれます so that the meaning remains the same. You need to change the subject and the last verb.**

1 私は やまだせんせいに かんじの よみかたを おしえて もらいました。
   やまだせんせいは、私に かんじの よみかたを おしえて くれました。

2 私は たなかさんに ジェームスさんを しょうかいして もらいました。
   _____

3 私は すずきさんに りょこうの しゃしんを 見せて もらいました。
   _____

4 私は ロバートさんに お金を かして もらいました。
   _____

5 私は ちちに あたらしい スーツを かって もらいました。
   _____

6 私は すずきさんに おいしい 日本りょうりを つくって もらいました。
   _____

F **Read the blog by Robert and answer the questions in Japanese.**

Daily Blog

今日は、たなかさんの うちへ はじめて あそびに 行きました。
たなかさんは あさくさに すんで います。きのう、ちずを かいて
もらいましたが、みちを まちがえて しまいましたから、たなかさんに
電話を かけて、あさくさえきまで 来て もらいました。たなかさんの
うちで、ジェームスさんに しょうかいして もらいました。それから、
ひるごはんを 食べて、たなかさんに よこはまへ つれて 行って
もらいました。よこはまは きれいな ところです。雨が ふって
いましたが、とても たのしかったです。

それから、たなかさんの うちへ かえって、ビールを 飲みました。
たなかさんの おくさんは、おいしい りょうりを つくって くれました。
つぎは、たなかさんに かまくらを あんないして もらいたいです。

1 たなかさんは　どこに　すんで　いますか。

_____

2 ロバートさんは　たなかさんの　うちの　行^いきかたが　分^わかりましたか。

_____

3 ロバートさんは　ジェームスさんを　しって　いましたか。

_____

4 ひるごはんを　食^たべて、どこへ　行^いきましたか。

_____

5 いい　天気^{てんき}でしたか。

_____

6 だれに　おいしい　りょうりを　つくって　もらいましたか。

_____

7 つぎは　どこへ　行^いきたいですか。

_____

| ちず | map |
| かまくら | Kamakura (a place near Tokyo) |

Vocabulary

G **Match the clothing items with the English translations. Then, choose the correct verbs to finish the sentences.**

1 くつ (*a*) を　はきます/~~きます~~。

2 コート _____ を　はきます/きます。

3 ジャケット _____ を　はきます/きます。

4 スカート _____ を　はきます/きます。

5 セーター _____ を　はきます/きます。

6 ズボン _____ を　はきます/きます。

7 ジーンズ _____ を　はきます/きます。

a shoes　**b** sweater　**c** jeans　**d** trousers　**e** coat　**f** skirt　**g** jacket

The particle に

So far, we have seen five uses of the particle に.

1 It can be attached to time expressions to mean *on* or *at*.

まいあさ　6時に　おきます。　　*I wake up at 6 a.m. every morning.*

2 It can be attached to place names when indicating that something or someone exists or lives there.

つくえの　上に　けいたいが　あります。　　*There is a mobile phone on the desk.*

3 It can be attached to the indirect object of verbs such as *give* in order to mean *to*.

ははに　しろい　はなを　あげました。　　*I gave my mother white flowers.*

4 It can be attached to the indirect object of verbs such as *receive* in order to mean *from*.

ちちに　あたらしい　スーツを　もらいました。　　*I got a new suit from my father.*

5 It is associated with a group of verbs that do not take the particle を, such as *meet, enter, become, sit,* etc.

ともだちに　あいます。　　*I (am) meet(ing) my friend.*

H **Decide which meaning the particle に has and match the correct number from the examples above.**

1 この　へやに　入っても　いいですか。(5)

2 ロバートさんは　たなかさんに　お金を　かりました。( )

3 たなかさんは　あさくさに　すんでいます。( )

4 やまだせんせいは　ロバートさんに　日本語を　おしえました。( )

5 火よう日に　すずきさんの　うちへ　行きました。( )

6 うちゅうひこうしに　なりたいです。( )

 # Writing

I Write a paragraph about your last Christmas. What did you give to others? What did others give to you? Be sure to express good will and gratitude by including what you did for others and what others did for you.

Japanese script

We will introduce four kanji in this unit.

Kanji	Reading	Meaning	Example words
先	さき、せん	*earlier, ahead*	<ruby>先生<rt>せんせい</rt></ruby> 先<ruby><rt>せん</rt></ruby>しゅう 先月 <ruby><rt>せんげつ</rt></ruby> *(last month)*
父	(お)とう(さん)、ちち	*father*	お父さん <ruby><rt>とう</rt></ruby> 父 <ruby><rt>ちち</rt></ruby>
母	(お)かあ(さん)、はは	*mother*	お母さん <ruby><rt>かあ</rt></ruby> 母 <ruby><rt>はは</rt></ruby>
白	しろ(い)、はく	*white*	白い はな <ruby><rt>しろ</rt></ruby> 白い ジャケット <ruby><rt>しろ</rt></ruby>

J Choose the correct kanji to complete the sentences.

先　　行　　話　　父　　日本語　　車　　白　　学校　　母　　先生　　学生

1 _____を　べんきょうして　います。

2 _____で、やまだ_____と　_____しました。

3 _____で　しぶやへ　_____きます。

4 たなかさんは　_____じゃ　ありません。

5 ロバートさんの　お_____さんと　お_____さんは　イギリスに　すんで　います。

6 _____しゅう、_____い　はなを　かいました。

 せんせい *literally means someone who was born before you, and it is used to address teachers, politicians and doctors.*

Self-check

Tick the box which matches your level of confidence.

1 = very confident   2 = need more practice   3 = not confident

下のボックスにじしんがあるかないかチェックしましょう。

1. じしんがある   2. れんしゅうがひつよう   3. じしんがない

	1	2	3
Expressing trying to do something (for the first time).			
Expressing completion of actions, often with regret.			
Expressing good will and gratitude.			
Identifying clothing terms.			
Using the particle に.			
Recognizing the kanji for *precedence*, *father*, *mother* and *white*.			

*For more information on conveying trying something for the first time and completion of actions using the て form refer to *Complete Japanese,* Units 9 and 11.

12 テレビを　みる　まえに　おふろに　はいります。

I have a bath before watching TV.

In this unit you will learn to:

✓ Form the plain form (present tense).

✓ Express sequences of actions.

✓ Describe your hobby.

✓ Express ability and possibility.

✓ Recognize the kanji for *listen, read, write* and *before*.

CEFR: Can summarize, report and give opinion about accumulated factual information on familiar matters with some confidence (B1); Can scan longer text in order to locate desired information in everyday material, such as letters, brochures and short official documents (B1).

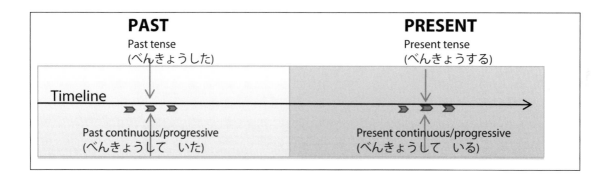

Meaning and usage

The plain form is called 'plain' as it does not carry politeness as, for example, the ます form does. It is used with friends and family members. The present tense of the plain form is also called the 'dictionary form' as this is the form we use for looking up verbs in a dictionary. In this unit, we will have a look at three uses of the plain form.

1 to describe sequences of actions, using 〜まえに (*before*):

かいしゃへ　行く　まえに、あさごはんを　食べます。 *I have breakfast before going to the office.*

テレビを　見る　まえに、おふろに　入ります。　 *I have a bath before watching TV.*

The tense of the sentence is determined by the final verb.

日本へ　来る　まえに、日本語を　べんきょうしました。 *I studied Japanese before coming to Japan.*

You can also use nouns and phrases that denote duration of time:

ばんごはんの　まえに　　　*before dinner*

3 (さん)ねんまえに　　　*three years ago*

2 to describe what your hobbies are, using 〜こと. By attaching こと to the plain form, you turn verbs into nouns:

しゅみは　おんがくを　きく　ことです。　　*My hobby is (listening to) music.*

しゅみは　テニスを　する　ことです。　　*My hobby is (playing) tennis.*

You can also use nouns in this structure.

しゅみは　おんがくです。　　*My hobby is music.*

しゅみは　テニスです。　　*My hobby is tennis.*

3 to describe ability, using the structure 〜ことが　できます (*be able to*):

ここで　けいたいを　つかう　ことが　できます。　　*You can use your mobile phone here.*

ここで　本を　かりる　ことが　できます。　　*You can borrow books here.*

Vocabulary

できます　II	*be able to, can*
ひきます　I	*play (stringed instruments)*
かきます　I	*draw (pictures)*
(〜に)　のぼります　I	*climb*
はらいます　I	*pay*
りょこうします　III	*travel*
しゅみ	*hobby*
え	*picture, drawing*
ピアノ	*piano*
やま	*mountain*
ふじさん	*Mt. Fuji*
カード	*credit card*
げん金	*cash*

How to form the plain form

Group I verbs

You need to change the last sound of the ます form stem from an 'i' sound to 'u' sound. The ます form can be divided into the stem and ます. In かいます, かい is the stem.

A Complete the table.

ます form	Plain form	English
かいます	かう	buy
あいます		meet
まちます	まつ	wait
	もつ	hold, carry
かえります	かえる	return
はいります		enter
飲みます		drink
	よむ	read
あそびます	あそぶ	play
えらびます		choose
	はたらく	work
行きます		go
	およぐ	swim
いそぎます		hurry
	話す	talk
けします		turn off

Group II verbs

You need to add る after the ます form stem.

B Complete the table.

ます form	Plain form	English
ねます	ねる	sleep
かけます		make (a phone call)
	食べる	eat
出かけます		go out
	見る	see, watch
かります		borrow
	おきる	wake up
きます		wear, put on

Group III verbs

C Complete the table.

ます form	Plain form	English
します	する	*do*
りょこうします		*travel*
	うんてんする	*drive*
来ます	来る	*come*

D Make a second sentence using まえに. It should have the same meaning as the original sentence.

1 おんがくを　きいて、ねます。

　ねる　まえに、おんがくを　ききます。

2 コーヒーを　飲んで、学校へ　行きます。

　_____

3 しんぶんを　よんで、ひるごはんを　食べます。

　_____

4 電話を　かけて、出かけます。

　_____

5 ブログを　かいて、おふろに　入ります。

　_____

6 メイルを　よんで、レポートを　かきます。

　_____

7 おふろに　入って、ビールを　飲みます。

　_____

E Complete the sentences by changing the verbs in brackets into the correct forms.

ロバート：　たなかさん、しゅみは　何ですか。

たなか：　やまに＿＿＿＿＿＿（のぼります）ことと、しゃしんを＿＿＿＿＿＿（とります）ことです。
　つまの　しゅみは　本を＿＿＿＿＿＿（よみます）ことです。ロバートさんは。

ロバート：　私の　しゅみは　えいがを＿＿＿＿＿＿（見ます）ことと、ギターを　＿＿＿＿＿＿（ひきます）
　ことです。

たなか： ロバートさん、すずきさんの しゅみを しって いますか。

ロバート： はい、しって います。すずきさんの しゅみは ＿＿＿＿＿＿＿（りょこうします）ことと、えを＿＿＿＿＿＿＿（かきます）ことです。すずきさんは えが とても 上手<ruby>上手<rt>じょうず</rt></ruby>です。

F　Complete the sentences by changing the verbs in brackets into the correct forms.

1　ロバートさんは <ruby>日本語<rt>にほんご</rt></ruby>を＿＿＿＿＿＿＿（<ruby>話<rt>はな</rt></ruby>します）が できます。

2　すずきさんは＿＿＿＿＿＿＿（およぎます）が できません。

3　<ruby>私<rt>わたし</rt></ruby>は パソコンを＿＿＿＿＿＿＿（つかいます）が できます。

4　<ruby>私<rt>わたし</rt></ruby>の <ruby>母<rt>はは</rt></ruby>は <ruby>日本<rt>にほん</rt></ruby>りょうりを＿＿＿＿＿＿＿（つくります）が できます。

5　7<ruby>月<rt>がつ</rt></ruby>から 9<ruby>月<rt>がつ</rt></ruby>まで、ふじさんに＿＿＿＿＿＿＿（のぼります）が できます。

6　やまだ<ruby>先生<rt>せんせい</rt></ruby>は ピアノを＿＿＿＿＿＿＿（ひきます）が できません。

7　ロバートさんは かんじを＿＿＿＿＿＿＿（よみます）が できます。

8　この みせでは、カードで＿＿＿＿＿＿＿（はらいます）が できません。
げん<ruby>金<rt>きん</rt></ruby>で はらって ください。

9　エドワードさんは ひらがなを＿＿＿＿＿＿＿（かきます）が できます。

Reading

G　Read the blog by Edward and answer the questions in Japanese.

📁 **PROFILE**

Like・Comment・Share

<ruby>3月<rt>がつ</rt></ruby><ruby>25日<rt>にち</rt></ruby>(<ruby>土<rt>ど</rt></ruby>)

3ねんまえに <ruby>日本<rt>にほん</rt></ruby>へ <ruby>来<rt>き</rt></ruby>ました。<ruby>今<rt>いま</rt></ruby>、コンピューターの かいしゃで はたらいて います。
<ruby>日本<rt>にほん</rt></ruby>の せいかつは いそがしいですが、とても たのしいです。
<ruby>日本語<rt>にほんご</rt></ruby>の べんきょうも して います。<ruby>日本語<rt>にほんご</rt></ruby>は むずかしいです。ひらがなと カタカナは
かく ことと よむ ことが できますが、かんじは あまり かく ことが できません。

<ruby>私<rt>わたし</rt></ruby>の しゅみは うんてんする ことと およぐ ことです。<ruby>今<rt>いま</rt></ruby>、<ruby>車<rt>くるま</rt></ruby>が ありませんから、
うんてんする ことが できませんが、まいしゅう ジムへ <ruby>行<rt>い</rt></ruby>って、およいで います。

1 エドワードさんは　いつ　日本へ　来ましたか。

_____

2 日本の　せいかつは　どうですか。

_____

3 エドワードさんは　ひらがなを　かく　ことが　できますか。

_____

4 エドワードさんの　しゅみは　何ですか。

_____

5 どうして　今　うんてんする　ことが　できませんか。

_____

6 まいしゅう　何を　して　いますか。

_____

H For each group of words, identify the odd one out.

1 びじゅつかん | ふじさん | え | しゃしん

2 月 | えいがかん | 学校 | かいしゃ

3 かりる | 来る | できる | きる

4 かえる | 入る | やる | 食べる

5 話す | する | かす | けす

6 ギター | カード | ピアノ | おんがく

 # Writing

I   Imagine you are going to introduce your best friend to your Japanese friend. Describe your best friend's appearance, personality, abilities and hobbies.

Japanese script

We will introduce four kanji in this unit.

Kanji	Reading	Meaning	Example words
聞	き(きます)、ぶん	listen, hear, ask	聞^ききます しん聞^{ぶん}
読	よ(みます)、どく	read	読^よみます
書	か(きます)、しょ	write	書^かきます 読書^{どくしょ} (reading)
前	まえ、ぜん	before, in front of	前^{まえ}に ご前^{ぜん} (morning, a.m.)

J Choose the correct kanji to complete the sentences.

| 食 | 先生 | 入 | 父 | 聞 | 前 | 書 | 読 | 白 |

1 ロバートさんは　ひらがなを_____く　ことが　できます。

2 やまだ_____に　かんじの_____みかたを　おしえて　もらいました。

3 _____の　しゅみは　おんがくを_____く　ことです。

4 すずきさんは_____い　ジャケットを　きて　います。

5 おふろに_____る_____に　ばんごはんを_____べます。

Self-check

Tick the box which matches your level of confidence.

　　1 = very confident　　　　2 = need more practice　　　　3 = not confident

下のボックスにじしんがあるかないかチェックしましょう。

　　1. じしんがある　　　　　2. れんしゅうがひつよう　　　　3. じしんがない

	1	2	3
Forming plain form (present tense).			
Expressing sequences of actions.			
Describing your hobby.			
Expressing ability and possibility.			
Recognizing the kanji for *listen, read, write* and *before*.			

*For more information on the plain form and its usages refer to *Complete Japanese,* Unit 10.

13 あたらしい　けいたいを　かう　つもりです。

I intend to buy a new mobile phone.

In this unit you will learn to:

✔ Express intentions.

✔ Express plans.

✔ Express causes and reasons.

✔ Express justifications.

✔ Recognize the kanji for *country*, *outside*, *friend* and *name*.

CEFR: Can write very brief reports to a standard, conventionalized format, which pass on routine factual information and state reasons for actions (B1); Can describe experiences and events, dreams, hopes and ambitions and briefly give reasons and explanations for opinions and plans (B1).

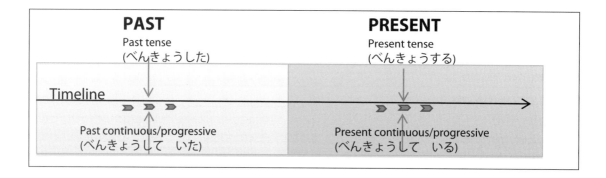

Meaning and usage

The present tense of the plain form is also used to express intentions, plans, reasons and justifications.

1　to express intentions, using 〜つもりです。つもり is a noun meaning *intention*:

らい
来しゅう、あたらしい　けいたいを　<u>かう</u>　つもりです。
I intend to buy a new mobile phone next week.

2　to express plans and schedules using 〜よていです。よてい means *schedule*:

しんかんせんは　9時に　<u>出る</u>　よていです。
The bullet train is due to depart at nine.

3 to express causes and reasons, using 〜ので. 〜ので is very similar to 〜から, attached to the end of sentences, but while the latter highlights the cause strongly, 〜ので presents causes and reasons more softly, so it is often used to ask for permissions or make excuses:

すみません、あたまが　いたいので、うちへ　かえっても　いいですか。
Excuse me, may I go home as I have a headache?

あしたは　土<ruby>と<rt>ど</rt></ruby>よう日<ruby>び<rt>び</rt></ruby>ですから、ぎん行<ruby>こう<rt>こう</rt></ruby>は　休<ruby>やす<rt>やす</rt></ruby>みです。
Because tomorrow is Saturday, banks are closed.

This expression can also be used with the plain forms of adjectives and nouns. When using な adjectives and nouns, you need to add な before ので.

あした　7時<ruby>じ<rt>じ</rt></ruby>から　しごとが　あるので、今日<ruby>きょう<rt>きょう</rt></ruby>は　はやく　ねます。
As I work from 7 a.m. tomorrow, I am going to bed early today.

いい　大学<ruby>だいがく<rt>だいがく</rt></ruby>に　入<ruby>はい<rt>はい</rt></ruby>りたいので、まい日<ruby>にち<rt>にち</rt></ruby>　べんきょうして　います。
I would like to go to a good university, so I study every day.

この　コンピューターは　高<ruby>たか<rt>たか</rt></ruby>いので、かう　ことが　できません。
This computer is expensive so I cannot buy it.

この　みせは　ゆうめいなので、人<ruby>ひと<rt>ひと</rt></ruby>が　おおいです。
As this shop is famous, many people are here.

ロバートさんは　イギリス人<ruby>じん<rt>じん</rt></ruby>なので　えい語<ruby>ご<rt>ご</rt></ruby>を　話<ruby>はな<rt>はな</rt></ruby>す　ことが　できます。
Robert is British, so he can speak English.

4 to express justifications using 〜んです or 〜のです. The former is used in spoken Japanese while the latter is used in formal (often written) Japanese. This expression can also be used with the plain forms of adjectives and nouns. When using な adjectives and nouns, you need to add な before んです or のです.

A: どうして　まい日<ruby>にち<rt>にち</rt></ruby>　べんきょうして　いますか。　　*Why do you study every day?*

B: いい　大学<ruby>だいがく<rt>だいがく</rt></ruby>に　入<ruby>はい<rt>はい</rt></ruby>りたいんです。　　*(It's because) I would like to go to a good university.*

いい　大学<ruby>だいがく<rt>だいがく</rt></ruby>に　入<ruby>はい<rt>はい</rt></ruby>って、すうがくを　べんきょうしたいのです。
(It's because) I would like to go to a good university and study Maths.

A Complete the table by choosing the correct words from the box.

> ことし　あした　先<small>せん</small>しゅう　先月<small>せんげつ</small>　きのう　来月<small>らいげつ</small>　来<small>らい</small>ねん　今<small>こん</small>しゅう

_____ (yesterday)	今日<small>きょう</small> (today)	_____ (tomorrow)
_____ (last week)	_____ (this week)	来<small>らい</small>しゅう (next week)
_____ (last month)	今月<small>こんげつ</small> (this month)	_____ (next month)
きょねん (last year)	_____ (this year)	_____ (next year)

Vocabulary

おわります	I	finish
はじまります	I	begin, start
やめます	II	quit, give up
ちょ金<small>きん</small>します	III	save money
ひっこしします	III	move (house)
どうして		why
がいこく		foreign country
ねつ		fever
かいぎ		meeting
ヨーロッパ		Europe
ベジタリアン		vegetarian

B Complete the sentences by changing the verbs in brackets.

1　来<small>らい</small>ねん　日本<small>にほん</small>へ_____（行<small>い</small>きます）つもりです。

2　日本<small>にほん</small>で　日本語<small>にほんご</small>を_____（べんきょうします）つもりです。

3　いちど　がいこくに_____（すんで　みます）つもりです。

4　つまに　プレゼントを_____（かって　あげます）つもりです。

5　こんばん　ともだちと_____（出<small>で</small>かけます）つもりです。

6　うちで、もう　いちど　父<small>ちち</small>と　母<small>はは</small>と_____（話<small>はな</small>します）つもりです。

C Complete the sentences by changing the verbs in brackets.

1 来月　ヨーロッパを＿＿＿＿＿＿＿＿（りょ行します）よていです。

2 あした　ふじさんに＿＿＿＿＿＿＿＿（のぼります）よていです。

3 来ねん＿＿＿＿＿＿＿＿（けっこんします）よていです。

4 かいぎは　5時に＿＿＿＿＿＿＿＿（おわります）よていです。

5 えいがは　7時に＿＿＿＿＿＿＿＿（はじまります）よていです。

6 来しゅうから　あたらしい　ITの　かいしゃで　＿＿＿＿＿＿＿＿（はたらきます）よていです。

D Complete the sentences by choosing the correct form.

1 あたまが＿＿＿＿＿＿＿＿、はやく　かえっても　いいですか。

   a　いたくて　　　　b　いたいので　　　c　いたいなので

2 今日は　おっとの＿＿＿＿＿＿＿＿、ホテルで　いっしょに　ばんごはんを　食べます。

   a　たんじょう日で　　b　たんじょう日ので　c　たんじょう日なので

3 すずきさんは　カラオケが＿＿＿＿＿＿＿＿、まいしゅう　行って　います。

   a　好きくて　　　　b　好きので　　　c　好きなので

4 あしたは　土よう日ですが、しごとが＿＿＿＿＿＿＿＿、あそびに　行く　ことが　できません。

   a　ありて　　　　b　あるので　　　c　あるなので

5 さいきん　まいばん　8時まで＿＿＿＿＿＿＿＿、うちに　10時に　かえります。

   a　はたらいて　いるので　b　はたらいて　いるなので　　c　はたらく　いるので

6 あした＿＿＿＿＿＿＿＿、いっしょに　あさくさへ　行きませんか。

   a　ひまで　　　　b　ひまので　　　c　ひまなので

E Complete the conversation by choosing the correct words from the box. You will need to change their forms.

| 見ます　　あります　　りょ行します　　すみたいです　　ベジタリアン　　てつだいます |

1 A: どうして　にくを　食べませんか。

  B: ＿＿＿＿＿＿＿＿んです。

2 A: どうして　ちょ金して　いますか。

  B: 来ねん　ヨーロッパを　＿＿＿＿＿＿＿＿んです。

3 A: どうして　はやく　かえりますか。

  B: ねつが＿＿＿＿＿＿＿＿んです。

4 A: どうして　かいしゃを　やめますか。

  B: 父の　しごとを＿＿＿＿＿＿＿＿んです。

5 **A:** どうして　ひっこししますか。

  B: 大きい　うちに_____んです。

6 **A:** どうして　パーティーに　来ませんか。

  B: こんばん　ともだちと　えいがを_____んです。

📖 Reading

F Read the email from Anne to Miss Suzuki and answer the questions in Japanese.

From:	
To:	
Subject:	

すずきさん、こんにちは!

さいきん　あつく　なりましたが、げんきですか。しごとは　どうですか。私は
げんきです。しごとは　いそがしいですが、　大さかの　せいかつは
たのしいです。

私は　来しゅうから　なつ休みなので、ともだちと　いっしょに　りょ行する
つもりです。ふじさんに　のぼる　よていです。それから　とうきょうへも　行く
よていです。とうきょうで　びじゅつかんへ　行く　つもりです。できれば、
とうきょうで　すずきさんと　ロバートさんと　たなかさんにも　あいたいです。
すずきさん、来しゅうの　日よう日、ひまですか。いっしょに　ばんごはんを
食べませんか。

へんじ　まって　います。

アン

1 アンさんは　どこに　すんで　いますか。

_____

2 アンさんの　しごとは　どうですか。

_____

3 今、きせつは　いつですか。

_____

4 アンさんは　来しゅう、何を　しますか。

_____

5 アンさんは　とうきょうで　何を　する　よていですか。

_____

6 アンさんは　いつ　すずきさんに　あいたいですか。

_____

げんきですか	_Are you well?_
できれば	_if possible_
へんじ	_reply_

 # Writing

G Imagine you have a friend living in Tokyo, and you are planning to go there for your summer holiday this year. Create an email to them, letting them know of your plans and suggest meeting them while you are there.

Japanese script

We will introduce four kanji in this unit.

Kanji	Reading	Meaning	Example words
国	くに、こく、ごく	country	<ruby>国<rt>くに</rt></ruby> お国 (your country)　<ruby>中国<rt>ちゅうごく</rt></ruby> <ruby>国語<rt>こくご</rt></ruby> (Japanese)
外	そと、がい	outside	<ruby>外国<rt>がいこく</rt></ruby> (foreign country)　<ruby>外国語<rt>がいこくご</rt></ruby> (foreign language)
友	とも、ゆう	friend	<ruby>友<rt>とも</rt></ruby>だち (friend)　<ruby>友人<rt>ゆうじん</rt></ruby> (friend)
名	な、めい	name	<ruby>名前<rt>なまえ</rt></ruby> (name)　ゆう<ruby>名<rt>めい</rt></ruby>

H Choose the correct kanji to complete the sentences.

名 国 書 見 友 名前 外国

1 いちど＿＿＿＿＿＿に　すんで　みたいです。

2 ＿＿＿だちと　いっしょに　えいがを＿＿＿＿ます。

3 <ruby>私<rt>わたし</rt></ruby>の＿＿＿＿＿は　イギリスです。

4 ＿＿＿＿＿を＿＿＿＿いて　ください。

5 この　みせは　ゆう＿＿＿＿です。

Self-check

Tick the box which matches your level of confidence.

1 = very confident　　　　2 = need more practice　　　　3 = not confident

下のボックスにじしんがあるかないかチェックしましょう。

1. じしんがある　　　　2. れんしゅうがひつよう　　　　3. じしんがない

	1	2	3
Expressing intentions.			
Expressing plans.			
Expressing causes and reasons.			
Expressing justifications.			
Recognizing the kanji for *country*, *outside*, *friend* and *name*.			

*For more information on the plain form and how to express intentions, plans, reasons and justifications refer to *Complete Japanese,* Unit 10.

14 わたしは にほんへ いった ことが あります。

I have been to Japan.

> **In this unit you will learn to:**
> ✅ Form the plain past tense.
> ✅ Express past experiences.
> ✅ Descirbe sequences of actions, using 〜あとで (after).
> ✅ Use frequency adverbs.
> ✅ Recognize the kanji for *mountain*, *year*, *interval* and *after*.

CEFR: Can write accounts of experiences, describing feelings and reactions in simple connected text (B1); Can fluently sustain a straightforward description of one of a variety of subjects of interest, presenting in a linear sequence of points (B1); Can read straightforward factual texts on subjects related to his field and interest with a satisfactory level of comprehension (B1).

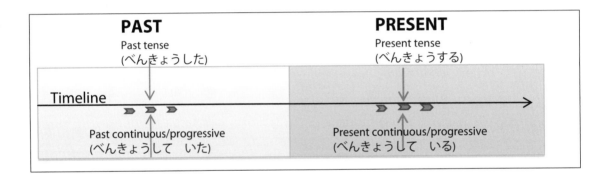

Meaning and usage

Past Tense

The past tense of the plain form is used for several functions. In this unit, we will look at two of them.

1 to describe past experiences with reference to the present, using 〜ことが あります. こと, as we saw in Unit 12, turns verbs into nouns:

私は 日本へ 行った ことが あります。   *I have been to Japan.*

私は さけを 飲んだ ことが ありません。   *I have never tried sake.*

The verb あります denotes possession/existence of things, as well as events taking place. So 私は 日本へ 行った ことが あります literally means *I have an experience of going to Japan.* The meaning and usage of this form is similar to that of perfect tense in English. Compare the following sentences:

私は　すしを　<u>食べた</u>　ことが　あります。　　*I have tried sushi.*

私は　きのう　すしを　食べました。　　　　*I had sushi yesterday.*

However, when the focus is on recently completed actions rather than past experiences, it is expressed with the simple past tense in Japanese, often with the adverb もう (meaning *already*).

ひるごはんは　もう　食べましたか。　　　　　*Have you had your lunch yet?*

はい、もう　食べました。　　　　　　　　　*Yes, I already have.*

You should not reply to the question above with はい、もう　食べた　ことが あります as it means *Yes, I have an experience of having lunch*, so it is not an appropriate answer in this context.

2　to describe sequences of actions, using ～ あとで (*after*). The tense of the sentence is determined by the final verb.

サッカーを　<u>した</u>　あとで　ビールを　飲みます。
I drink beer after playing football.

しごとが　<u>おわった</u>　あとで　えいがを　見ました。
I saw a film after finishing work.

You can also use nouns for this form. You need to add の after nouns.

<u>しごとの</u>　あとで　えいがを　見ました。　*I saw a film after work.*

Care should be taken when the answer to the question above is negative. As we saw in Unit 10, to describe things you haven't done yet or are still in process of doing, the present continuous form is used:

いいえ、まだ　食べて　いません。
No I haven't yet.

A あとで B is very similar to A てから B (て form plus から). The former emphasizes the order in which events happen. The latter is used when the first action is a precondition of the second action.

How to form the plain past tense

In order to form the plain past tense, simply change て and で of the て form into た and だ respectively.

A Complete the table.

Group I

ます form	て form	Plain past tense	English
かいます	かって	かった	buy
つかいます	つかって		use
まちます		まった	wait
もちます	もって		hold, carry
かえります	かえって		return
のぼります		のぼった	climb
飲みます	飲んで	飲んだ	drink
休みます	休んで		rest
あそびます		あそんだ	play
えらびます	えらんで		choose
しにます	しんで		die
はたらきます	はたらいて	はたらいた	work
聞きます	聞いて		listen
行きます		行った	go
およぎます	およいで	およいだ	swim
いそぎます	いそいで		hurry
話します	話して		talk
かします		かした	lend

> *Remember that the verb* 行きます *is an exception to the normal rules for conjugating Group I verbs.*

B Complete the sentences by changing the verbs in brackets.

1 私は　かぞくと　日本へ　＿＿＿＿＿＿＿＿（行きます）　ことが　あります。

2 たなかさんは　やまだ先生と　ふじさんに　＿＿＿＿＿＿＿＿（のぼります）　ことが　あります。

3 たなかさんは　2ねんかん　外国に　＿＿＿＿＿＿＿＿（すみます）　ことが　あります。

4 日本の　さけを　＿＿＿＿＿＿＿＿（飲みます）　ことが　ありません。

5 えきで　友だちを　3時かん　＿＿＿＿＿＿＿＿（まちます）　ことが　あります。

6 ゆう名な　はいゆうに　＿＿＿＿＿＿＿＿（あいます）　ことが　ありません。

～かん	duration
2ねんかん	two years
3時かん	three hours

C Complete the table.

Group II

ます form	て form	Plain past tense	English
ねます	ねて	ねた	sleep
食べます	食べて		eat
見せます	見せて		show
おしえます		おしえた	teach
わすれます	わすれて		forget
出かけます	出かけて		go out
かんがえます		かんがえた	think, consider
おきます	おきて	おきた	wake up
見ます	見て		see
います		いた	be
かります	かりて		borrow

D Complete the table.

ます form	て form	Plain past tense	English
します	して	した	do
りょ行します	りょ行して		travel
べんきょうします	べんきょうして		study
せつめいします		せつめいした	explain
来ます	来て		come

E Complete the sentences by changing the verbs in brackets.

1 私は　ヨーロッパを＿＿＿＿＿＿＿＿（りょ行します）　ことが　あります。

2 ロバートさんは　すもうを＿＿＿＿＿＿＿＿（見ます）　ことが　ありません。

3 おいしい　日本の　りょうりを＿＿＿＿＿＿＿＿（食べます）　ことが　あります。

4 イギリスで　電車に　パスポートを＿＿＿＿＿＿＿＿（わすれます）　ことが
あります。

5 エドワードさんは　ぜんぜん　スキーを＿＿＿＿＿＿＿＿（します）　ことが
ありません。

6 前<ruby>に<rt>まえ</rt></ruby>　いちど　ここへ＿＿＿＿＿＿＿（来<ruby><rt>き</rt></ruby>ます）　ことが　あります。

F Complete the sentences by changing the verbs in brackets. Is it 〜ことが
あります, 〜ました or 〜ていません?

たなか:　　　エドワードさん、しゅみは　何<ruby><rt>なん</rt></ruby>ですか。

エドワード:　しゅみは　りょ行<ruby><rt>こう</rt></ruby>する　ことです。

たなか:　　　そうですか。大<ruby><rt>おお</rt></ruby>さかへ　**1**＿＿＿＿＿（行<ruby><rt>い</rt></ruby>きます）ことが　ありますか。

エドワード:　はい、何<ruby><rt>なん</rt></ruby>かいか　**2**＿＿＿＿＿＿（行<ruby><rt>い</rt></ruby>きます）ことが　あります。

　　　　　　　きょうとと　ならへも　**3**＿＿＿＿＿＿（行<ruby><rt>い</rt></ruby>きます）。おきなわは

　　　　　　　4＿＿＿＿＿＿＿（行<ruby><rt>い</rt></ruby>きます）ことが　ありません。

たなか:　　　そうですか。ところで　もう　レポートを

　　　　　　　5＿＿＿＿＿＿＿（書<ruby><rt>か</rt></ruby>きます）か。エドワード:はい。

たなか:　　　ひるごはんは　もう　**6**＿＿＿＿＿＿（食<ruby><rt>た</rt></ruby>べます）か。

エドワード:　いいえ、まだ　**7**＿＿＿＿＿＿＿（食<ruby><rt>た</rt></ruby>べます）。

たなか:　　　じゃ、いっしょに　食<ruby><rt>た</rt></ruby>べましょう。

何<ruby><rt>なん</rt></ruby>かいか	*few times*
ところで	*by the way*
おきなわ	*Okinawa*

G Create sentences using the phrases given.

1 サッカーを　しました　→　おふろに　入<ruby><rt>はい</rt></ruby>りました
　　サッカーを　した　あとで、おふろに　入<ruby><rt>はい</rt></ruby>りました。

2 ばんごはんを　食<ruby><rt>た</rt></ruby>べました　→　テレビを　見<ruby><rt>み</rt></ruby>ました

＿＿＿＿＿＿＿＿＿＿＿＿＿＿＿＿＿＿＿＿＿＿

3 メイルを　読<ruby><rt>よ</rt></ruby>みます　→　レポートを　書<ruby><rt>か</rt></ruby>きます

＿＿＿＿＿＿＿＿＿＿＿＿＿＿＿＿＿＿＿＿＿＿

4 べんきょうしました　→　CDを　聞<ruby><rt>き</rt></ruby>きました

＿＿＿＿＿＿＿＿＿＿＿＿＿＿＿＿＿＿＿＿＿＿

5 おふろに 入ります → ビールを 飲みます

_____

6 しごとが おわります → カラオケに 行きます

_____

Vocabulary

Expressions for frequency

Frequency expressions are often used when expressing experiences.

前に	*before*
いちど	*once*
何かいか	*few times*
いちども　〜ません	*not even once*
あまり　〜ません	*not often*
ぜんぜん　〜ません	*not at all*

H Using the activities given and the frequency expressions above, create sentences describing what Edward has or has not done.

1 日本の りょうりを 食べます・あまり

エドワードさんは あまり 日本の りょうりを 食べた ことが ありません。

2 大さかへ 行きます・何かいか

_____

3 スキーを します・いちども

_____

4 中学校で はたらきます・前に

_____

5 日本の おさけを 飲みます・ぜんぜん

_____

6 ふじさんに のぼります・いちど

_____

📖 Reading

I Read the following text about Edward's experience and answer the questions in Japanese.

エドワード・キングさんは　25さいの　イギリス人です。今、コンピューターの

かいしゃで　はたらいて　います。しゅみは　りょ行です。はじめての

かい外りょ行は　フランスでした。今までに　アメリカ、ヨーロッパ、そして

アジアへ　行った　ことが　ありますが、アフリカへは　いちども　行った

ことが　ありません。

エドワードさんは　日本の　小さい　中学校で　えい語の　きょうしとして

はたらいた　ことが　あります。2ねんかん　はたらきました。なつ休みに

友だちと　ふじさんに　のぼった　ことも　あります。すもうを　見に　行った

ことも　あります。おんせんに　入った　ことも　あります。どれも　たのしい

おもい出です。

1 エドワードさんは　今　どこで　はたらいて　いますか。

_____

2 今までに　どこへ　りょ行した　ことが　ありますか。

_____

3 日本の　中学校で　何を　した　ことが　ありますか。

_____

4 友だちと　何を　した　ことが　ありますか。

_____

かい外りょ行	*travelling abroad*
～として	*as ～*
おんせん	*hot spring*
どれも	*all*
おもい出	*memory*

 # Writing

J **What experiences do you have? Imagine you are at your Japanese friend's party and meeting new people. Tell them about work, travel and other experiences using ～ことが　あります、 ～ことが　ありません as well as expressions for frequency. For example, have you been to Japan? If so, where did you go? If not, where would you like to go? Have you ever tried sushi? Make sure to include how you felt about them.**

Japanese script

We will introduce four kanji in this unit.

Kanji	Reading	Meaning	Example words
山	やま、さん	*mountain*	<ruby>山<rt>やま</rt></ruby> <ruby>ふじ山<rt>さん</rt></ruby>
年	とし、ねん	*year*	<ruby>今年<rt>ことし</rt></ruby> <ruby>来年<rt>らいねん</rt></ruby>
間	あいだ、かん	*interval, between*	<ruby>3年間<rt>ねんかん</rt></ruby> (three years) <ruby>1時間<rt>じかん</rt></ruby> (one hour)
後	あと、うし(ろ)、ご	*after, later, behind*	<ruby>後で<rt>あと</rt></ruby> <ruby>ご後<rt>ご</rt></ruby> (afternoon, p.m.)

K Choose the correct kanji to complete the sentences.

時間	来年	外国	前	後	山	行	飲	友

1 エドワードさんは　コンピューターの　かいしゃで　はたらく＿＿＿＿＿に、
　<ruby>中学校で<rt>ちゅうがっこう</rt></ruby>　はたらいた　ことが　あります。

2 えきで　1＿＿＿＿＿　＿＿＿＿＿だちを　まちました。

3 しごとが　おわった＿＿＿＿＿で　ビールを＿＿＿＿＿みます。

4 すずきさんは＿＿＿＿＿へ＿＿＿＿＿った　ことが　ありません。

5 ふじ＿＿＿＿＿に　のぼった　ことが　あります。

6 ＿＿＿＿＿イギリスへ　かえります。

Self-check

Tick the box which matches your level of confidence.

1 = very confident   2 = need more practice   3 = not confident

下のボックスにじしんがあるかないかチェックしましょう。

1. じしんがある   2. れんしゅうがひつよう   3. じしんがない

	1	2	3
Forming the plain past tense.			
Expressing past experiences.			
Describing sequences of actions, using 〜あとで (*after*).			
Using frequency adverbs.			
Recognizing the kanji for *mountain*, *year*, *interval* and *after*.			

*For more information on the plain past form and how to express experiences and sequences of actions refer to *Complete Japanese,* Unit 11.

15 タクシーで　いった　ほうが　いいですよ。

You'd better take a taxi.

In this unit you will learn to:

- ✓ List some (representative) actions among many other actions.
- ✓ Give advice.
- ✓ Make comparisons.
- ✓ Say *when*, using とき.
- ✓ Recognize the kanji for *noon*, *every*, *river* and *sea*.

CEFR: Can write accounts of experiences, describing feelings and reactions in simple connected text (B1); Can identify the main conclusions in clearly signaled argumentative texts; Can recognize the line of argument in the treatment of the issue presented, but not necessarily in detail (B1); Can make his opinions and reactions understood as regards solutions to problems or practical questions (B1).

Meaning and usage

In this unit, we will look at how to list some representative actions and how to give advice using the plain past tense. We will also look at how to make comparisons and how to express time references using *when*.

1   to list some (representative) actions among many other actions in a random order, using 〜た(だ)り 〜た(だ)り　します. The tense of the whole sentence is determined by the final verb:

日よう日に　テレビを　見たり、おんがくを　聞いたり　します。
On Sundays I watch TV, listen to music and so on.

日よう日に　テレビを　見たり、おんがくを　聞いたり　しました。
Last Sunday I watched TV, listened to music and so on.

Compare this sentence pattern with sentences that contains the て form to express sequences of actions. The difference is that the order of actions is rigid in the latter, while the former does not express a sequence of actions, and implies that there may be more actions.

日よう日に　テレビを　見て、おんがくを　聞きました。
Last Sunday I watched TV and then listened to music.

2   to give advice, using the plain past tense with 〜ほうが　いいです. This literally means 〜 *is better*.

タクシーで　行った　ほうが　いいですよ。　*You'd better take a taxi.*

いそいだ　ほうが　いいですよ。　*You should hurry.*

 When よ is added at the end of sentences, it gives more emphasis to the advice.

Vocabulary

そうじします　III	clean (a room)
せんたくします　III	wash (clothes)
いります　I	need, require
つかれます　II	be tired
子ども	child
ミュージカル	musical
びょういん	hospital
くすり	medicine
くすりを　飲みます	take medicine
ポップコーン	popcorn
手がみ	letter
うみ	sea
かわ	river
ご前	a.m.
ご後	p.m.
はやい	quick, early
わかい	young

A **Complete the sentences by changing the verbs in brackets.**

1 友だちと＿＿＿＿＿＿＿（飲みます）り＿＿＿＿＿＿＿（食べます）り　しました。

2 なつ休みに　山に＿＿＿＿＿＿＿（のぼります）り　かわで＿＿＿＿＿＿＿（およぎます）り　しました。

3 先しゅうの　土よう日に　テニスを＿＿＿＿＿＿＿（します）り　えいがを　＿＿＿＿＿＿＿（見ます）り
しました。

4 まいしゅう　日よう日に　子どもと＿＿＿＿＿＿＿（あそびます）り　かぞくと
＿＿＿＿＿＿＿＿（出かけます）り　します。

5 かいしゃで　メイルを＿＿＿＿＿＿＿（読みます）り　レポートを　＿＿＿＿＿＿＿（書きます）り　します。

6 ロンドンで　びじゅつかんへ＿＿＿＿＿＿＿（行きます）り　ミュージカルを　＿＿＿＿＿＿＿（見ます）り
しました。

B Turn the sentences into advice.

1 びょういんへ　行きます。

　　びょういんへ　行った　ほうが　いいですよ。

2 くすりを　飲みます。

_____

3 たばこを　やめます。

_____

4 まいあさ　あさごはんを　食べます。

_____

5 すこし　休みます。

_____

6 はやく　ねます。

_____

How to make comparisons

It was noted earlier that 〜ほうが　いいです literally means 〜 *is better*. You can use this pattern to make comparisons between two things as well. In English, when comparing two things, adjectives change their forms (such as *bigger, smaller*, etc.). In Japanese, adjectives do not change. Instead, the items that 'win' the comparison are marked with ほうが and the items that 'lose' the comparison are marked with より.

バス<u>より</u>　電車の　<u>ほうが</u>　はやいです。　　*Trains are faster than buses.*

この　ラップトップ<u>より</u>　あの　ラップトップの　<u>ほうが</u>　高いです。
That laptop is more expensive than this laptop.

Notice you need to add の before ほうが when comparing two nouns. When comparing actions, plain forms are used and you do not need to add の.

バスで　<u>行くより</u>　電車で　<u>行く</u>　<u>ほうが</u>　はやいです。
Going by train is faster than going by bus.

C **Make comparisons using the information given, then give the English translation.**

1 山 ＜ うみ （好き）
山より　うみの　ほうが　好きです。

I prefer the sea to mountains.

2 たなかさん　＜　ロバートさん　（せが　高い）

_____

_____

3 ロバートさん　＜　すずきさん　（わかい）

_____

_____

4 えいが　＜　本　（おもしろい）

_____

_____

5 ご前　＜　ご後　（ひま）

_____

_____

6 ロンドン　＜　とうきょう　（人が　おおい）

_____

_____

7 すずきさん　＜　やまだ先生　（げん気）

_____

_____

8 手がみを　書きます　＜　メイルを　書きます　（べんり）

_____

_____

How to say *when*, using 〜とき

とき is attached after plain forms (past and present) to mean *when*, as in the following examples:

中国に　すんで　いた　とき、中国語を　べんきょうして　いました。
ちゅうごく　　　　　　　　　　　　　　　ちゅうごくご

When I was living in China, I was studying Chinese.

You can also use とき with nouns and adjectives. When using it with nouns, you need to add の, and when you use it with な adjectives, you need to add な. You do not need to change anything when you use it with い adjectives.

子どもの　とき、父と　よく　こうえんへ　あそびに　行きました。
こ　　　　　　　ちち　　　　　　　　　　　　　　　　　　い

When I was a child, I often went to the park to play with my father.

ひまな　とき、うちで　おんがくを　聞いたり　本を　読んだり　します。
　　　　　　　　　　　　　　　　　　き　　　　ほん　　よ

When I have free time, I do things such as listening to music and reading a book.

あたまが　いたい　とき、くすりを　飲みます。
　　　　　　　　　　　　　　　の

When I have a headache, I take medicine.

You need to be careful when using the plain form (past and present) of verbs in this structure. When the present tense is attached to とき, it indicates that the action has not been completed, while when past tense is attached, it signifies the action has been completed. Compare the following two sentences:

イギリスへ　行く　とき、ロバートさんに　あいました。
　　　　　い

I saw Robert when I went (while I was going) to the UK.

イギリスへ　行った　とき、ロバートさんに　あいました。
　　　　　い

I saw Robert when I went to the UK.

The first sentence with the present tense indicates I saw Robert before I reached the UK, while the second sentence with the past tense indicates I had reached the UK when I saw Robert.

D Complete the sentences by choosing the correct option.

1 _____とき、あまり　べんきょうしませんでした。
　　a 学生　　　　　　　b 学生な　　　　　　　c 学生の
　　　がくせい　　　　　　　　がくせい　　　　　　　　がくせい

2 _____とき、たくさん　プレゼントを　もらいました。
　　a けっこんした　　b けっこんしたの　　c けっこんします

3 えいがを_____ とき、ポップコーンを　食べます。
　　　　　　　　　　　　　　　　　　　　　　　　た
　　a 見ます　　　　　b 見る　　　　　　　c 見るの
　　　み　　　　　　　　み　　　　　　　　　み

4 ねつが_____ とき、かいしゃを　休んだ　ほうが　いいです。
　　　　　　　　　　　　　　　　　　　やす
　　a あります　　　　b あるの　　　　　　c ある

5 _____とき、ぜんぜん　ちょ金しませんでした。
　　　　　　　　　　　　　　　　　　きん
　　a わかい　　　　　b わかいの　　　　　c わかいな

E Choose the correct tense of the verb to complete the sentences.

1 外国へ　（りょ行する | りょ行した）とき、パスポートが　いります。

2 イタリアへ　（りょ行する | りょ行した）とき、しゃしんを　たくさん　とりました。

3 おさけを　（飲む | 飲んだ）とき、車を　うんてんしては　いけません。

4 うちを　（出る | 出た）とき、テレビを　けしました。

5 うちへ　（かえる | かえった）とき、ケーキを　かいました。

6 ふじ山へ　（のぼる | のぼった）とき、すこし　つかれました。

Reading

F Read the text describing Mr Tanaka's life so far, then answer the questions in Japanese.

	たなかさんは　子どもの　とき、こうちに　すんで　いました。よく　山に　のぼったり、
	うみで　およいだり　しました。かぞくと　とうきょうや　大さかへ　行った　ことも
	あります。中学校へ　行って　いた　ときは　きょうしに　なりたかったです。
	大さかの　大学に　入ったので、大学生の　ときは　大さかに　すんで　いました。
	大学生の　とき、たなかさんは　あまり　べんきょうしませんでした。いつも　友だちと
	飲みに　行ったり、アルバイトを　したり　して　いましたから。そのころ、たなかさんは、
	おくさんの　かずこさんに　あいました。
	大学を　出た　後で、とうきょうの　ITの　かいしゃに　入りました。かいしゃに　入って
	3年後に、かずこさんと　けっこんしました。今、子どもが　ふたり　います。しごとは
	いそがしくて　たいへんですが、とうきょうの　せいかつは　とても　たのしいです。ひまな
	とき、よく　子どもと　あそんだり、おくさんと　出かけたり　して　います。

1 たなかさんは　子どもの<ruby>子<rt>こ</rt></ruby>　とき、どこに　すんで　いましたか。

_____

2 たなかさんは　子どもの<ruby>子<rt>こ</rt></ruby>　とき、よく　<ruby>何<rt>なに</rt></ruby>を　しましたか。

_____

3 <ruby>大学生<rt>だいがくせい</rt></ruby>の　とき、どうして　あまり　べんきょうしませんでしたか。

_____

4 いつ　かずこさんと　けっこんしましたか。

_____

5 たなかさんは　<ruby>今<rt>いま</rt></ruby>、ひまな　とき、<ruby>何<rt>なに</rt></ruby>を　しますか。

_____

こうち	_Kouchi prefecture (a place in Shikoku island)_
アルバイト	_part-time job_
そのころ	_around that time_
〜<ruby>年後<rt>ねんご</rt></ruby>	_after 〜 years_

Vocabulary

G **For each group of words, identify the odd one out.**

   1 いしゃ | <ruby>学生<rt>がくせい</rt></ruby> | びょういん | くすり

   2 うみ | <ruby>山<rt>やま</rt></ruby> | かわ | みせ

   3 そうじ | せんたく | べんきょう | りょうり

   4 ご<ruby>前<rt>ぜん</rt></ruby> | とけい | ご<ruby>後<rt>ご</rt></ruby> | けいたい

   5 わかい | <ruby>男<rt>おとこ</rt></ruby>の<ruby>子<rt>こ</rt></ruby> | <ruby>女<rt>おんな</rt></ruby>の<ruby>子<rt>こ</rt></ruby> | <ruby>子<rt>こ</rt></ruby>ども

 # Writing

H Describe your life so far to your friends. Make sure to include where you used to live when you were a child using 子どもの　とき, what you routinely did or enjoyed doing, using ～た(だ)り、 ～た(だ)り, and what you wanted to become using ～になりたかったです. Also describe what you were like when you were a student, what you used to do with your friends, etc. End the description with what you normally do when you have free time.

Japanese script

We will introduce four kanji in this unit.

Kanji	Reading	Meaning	Example words
午	ご	*noon*	ご 午後 ごぜん 午前
毎	まい	*every, each*	まいにち　　まいとし　　まいつき　　まいとし 毎日、　毎年、　毎月、　毎年 まい　　　　　まい　　　　まい 毎しゅう、　毎あさ、　毎ばん
川	かわ、がわ	*river*	かわ 川で　およぎます がわ テームズ川
海	うみ、かい	*sea*	うみ 海で　およぎます にほんかい 日本海

I **Choose the correct kanji to complete the sentences.**

毎年　　本　　午　　山　　行　　毎　　海　　川　　午　　休　　読　　前　　川

1 _____前 より_____後 のほうが　ひまです。

2 _____あさ　あさごはんを　食べた　ほうが　いいですよ。

3 テームズ_____は　ゆう名な_____です。

4 スペインへ 行って、かぞくと_____で　およぎました。

5 なつ_____みに_____に　のぼりました。

6 _____ クリスマスに　イギリスへ_____きます。

7 ねる_____に_____を_____みます。

Self-check

Tick the box which matches your level of confidence.

1 = very confident   2 = need more practice   3 = not confident

下のボックスにじしんがあるかないかチェックしましょう。

1. じしんがある   2. れんしゅうがひつよう   3. じしんがない

	1	2	3
Listing some (representative) actions among many other actions.			
Giving advice.			
Making comparisons.			
Saying *when*, using とき.			
Recognizing the kanji for *noon, every, river* and *sea*.			

*For more information on the plain past form and how to list some (representative) actions among many other actions in random order, how to give advice, how to make comparisons and how to say *when* refer to *Complete Japanese*, Unit 11.

こんばん　すしを　たべようか。

Shall we have sushi tonight?

In this unit you will learn to:

✓ Form the plain volitional form.

✓ Express suggestions in plain style conversations.

✓ Express what the speaker is thinking of doing.

✓ Express trying to do something but failing to do so.

✓ Use the particle が.

✓ Recognize the kanji for *one, two, three* and *four*.

CEFR: Can make his opinions and reactions understood as regards solutions to problems or practical questions (B1); Can develop an argument well enough to be followed without difficulty most of the time; Can explain why something is a problem (B1); Can write very brief reports to a standard, conventionalized format, which pass on routine factual information and state reasons for actions (B1).

Meaning and usage

The volitional form is used in plain style conversations to express decisions, suggestions, and also to express the intention to do something.

1 to express suggestions in plain style conversations:

今ばん、すしを　**食べよう**か。　*Shall we have sushi tonight?*

うん、**食べよう**。　　*Yes, let's.*

This form is also used when talking to or about yourself to mean *I will*.

今日は　はやく　**かえろう**。　*I will go home early today.*

あしたは　何を　**しよう**か。　*What shall I do tomorrow?*

2 to express what the speaker is thinking of doing, using 〜と　おもって　います. おもって　います is the continuous form of おもいます and it indicates that the speaker has been thinking about doing something for some time:

来年　イギリスへ　**行こう**と　おもって　います。
I am thinking of going to the UK next year.

すずきさんは　あたらしい　くつを　**かおう**と
おもって　います。
Miss Suzuki is thinking of buying new shoes.

> 🍎 *Notice that pronouns (I, you, he/she) are often left out of Japanese sentences. This means that it is important to understand the context in which a sentence is written or spoken.*

We have learnt similar expressions previously: 〜たいです (in Unit 4, meaning *want to*) and 〜つもりです (in Unit 13, meaning *intend to*). Compare the difference in meaning:

来年　イギリスへ　行きたいです。　　*I want to go to the UK next year.*

来年　イギリスへ　行こうと　おもって　います。

I am thinking of going to the UK next year.

来年　イギリスへ　行く　つもりです。

I intend to/am planning to go to the UK next year.

 These examples are in order of certainty with 〜つもりです being the most definite plan.

3 to express trying to do something but failing to do so, using volitional form plus 〜と　します:

きょ年　中国語を　**ならおうと**　しましたが、むずかしかったので、やめました。

I tried to learn Chinese last year but as it was difficult, I gave up.

You have learnt how to say *give something a try* using 〜て　みます, which does not imply failing to do something. Compare the difference in meaning:

中国語を　ならおうと　しました。　　*I tried to learn Chinese (and it was unsuccessful).*

中国語を　ならって　みました。　　*I had a go at learning Chinese.*

How to form the plain volitional form

Group I verbs

You need to change the last sound of the ます form stem from *i* to *o* and add う.

A Complete the table.

ます form	Plain form	English
かいます	かおう	*buy*
あいます		*meet*
まちます	まとう	*wait*
	もとう	*hold, carry*
かえります	かえろう	*return*
入ります		*enter*
飲みます		*drink*
	読もう	*read*
あそびます	あそぼう	*play*
えらびます		*choose*
	はたらこう	*work*
行きます		*go*
	およごう	*swim*
いそぎます		*hurry*
	話そう	*talk*
けします		*turn off*

B Complete the sentences by changing the verbs to the volitional form. Then, give the English translation.

1 今ばん、いっしょに　飲もう(飲みます)。

   Let's drink together tonight.

2 つかれたから、ちょっと ＿＿＿＿＿＿＿＿(休みます)。

   ＿＿＿＿＿＿＿＿＿＿＿＿＿＿＿＿＿＿＿＿＿

3 あしたは　はやく　学校へ ＿＿＿＿＿＿＿(行きます)。

   ＿＿＿＿＿＿＿＿＿＿＿＿＿＿＿＿＿＿＿＿＿

4 今ばん　6時に　えきで ＿＿＿＿＿＿＿＿＿ (あいます)。

   ＿＿＿＿＿＿＿＿＿＿＿＿＿＿＿＿＿＿＿＿＿

5 この　リポートを ＿＿＿＿＿＿＿＿(書いて　しまいます)。

   ＿＿＿＿＿＿＿＿＿＿＿＿＿＿＿＿＿＿＿＿＿

6 来しゅう　大さかへ ＿＿＿＿＿＿＿＿＿(あそびに　行きます)。

   ＿＿＿＿＿＿＿＿＿＿＿＿＿＿＿＿＿＿＿＿＿

Group II verbs

You need to add よう after the ます form stem.

C Complete the table.

ます form	Plain form	English
ねます	ねよう	*sleep*
かけます		*make (a phone call)*
	食べよう	*eat*
でかけます		*go out*
	見よう	*see, watch*
かります		*borrow*
	おきよう	*wake up*
きます		*wear, put on*

Group III verbs

D Complete the table.

ます form	Plain form	English
します	しよう	*do*
りょ行します		*travel*
	うんてんしよう	*drive*
来ます	来よう	*come*

E Complete the sentences by changing the verbs to the volitional form. Then, give the English translation.

1 ばんごはんの　後で、えいがを　見よう(見ます)。

Let's watch a film after dinner.

2 1時から　5時まで＿＿＿＿＿＿＿＿＿＿＿＿(べんきょうします)。

＿＿＿＿＿＿＿＿＿＿＿＿＿＿＿＿＿＿＿＿＿＿＿＿＿＿＿＿＿＿＿＿＿＿

3 来しゅう　また　ここへ＿＿＿＿＿＿＿＿＿(来ます)。

＿＿＿＿＿＿＿＿＿＿＿＿＿＿＿＿＿＿＿＿＿＿＿＿＿＿＿＿＿＿＿＿＿＿

4 この　ワインを＿＿＿＿＿＿＿＿＿＿＿(かって　みます)。

＿＿＿＿＿＿＿＿＿＿＿＿＿＿＿＿＿＿＿＿＿＿＿＿＿＿＿＿＿＿＿＿＿＿

5 ロバートさんに　プレゼントを＿＿＿＿＿＿＿＿＿(あげます)。

＿＿＿＿＿＿＿＿＿＿＿＿＿＿＿＿＿＿＿＿＿＿＿＿＿＿＿＿＿＿＿＿＿＿

6 あした　いっしょに＿＿＿＿＿＿＿＿＿(出かけます)。

＿＿＿＿＿＿＿＿＿＿＿＿＿＿＿＿＿＿＿＿＿＿＿＿＿＿＿＿＿＿＿＿＿＿

F Complete the sentences by changing the verbs to the appropriate form.

1 来年　ヨーロッパを＿＿＿＿＿＿＿＿＿＿＿（りょ行します）と　おもって　います。

2 かいしゃを＿＿＿＿＿＿＿＿＿（やめます）て、父の　しごとを＿＿＿＿＿＿＿＿＿＿（てつだいます）と　お
もって　います。

3 日よう日に＿＿＿＿＿＿＿＿＿（そうじします）り、＿＿＿＿＿＿＿＿＿＿＿（せんたくし
ます）り＿＿＿＿＿＿＿＿＿＿（します）と　おもって　います。

4 ＿＿＿＿＿＿＿＿＿＿（はたらきます）ながら　大学へ＿＿＿＿＿＿＿＿＿＿（行きます）とおもって　います。

5 今ばん＿＿＿＿＿＿＿＿＿（ねます）前に　メイルを＿＿＿＿＿＿＿＿＿（書きます）と　おもって　います。

6 友だちと　えいがを＿＿＿＿＿＿＿＿＿（見ます）後で　レストランで　ばんごは
んを＿＿＿＿＿＿＿＿＿（食べます）と　おもって　います。

G Choose the correct verbs and change them into the volitional form to complete the sentences.

わすれます、りょ行します、書きます、やめます

1 たなかさんは　今までに　何かいか　たばこを＿＿＿＿＿＿＿＿＿＿と　しましたが、まだ　すって
います。

2 学生の　とき、ヨーロッパを＿＿＿＿＿＿＿＿＿＿と　しましたが、お金が

あまり　ありませんでしたから、中国へ　行きました。

3 すずきさんは　前の　ボーイフレンドを＿＿＿＿＿＿＿＿＿＿と　しましたが、わすれる　ことが　でき
ませんでした。

4 きのう　レポートを＿＿＿＿＿＿＿＿＿＿と　しましたが、ぜんぜん　時間が　ありませんでした。

📖 Reading

H Read the following conversation between Mr Tanaka and Miss Suzuki about their New Year's resolutions and answer the questions in Japanese.

すずき: たなかさん、あけまして　おめでとう　ございます。

たなか: あけまして　おめでとう　ございます。すずきさん、今年の　ほうふは
何ですか。

すずき: そうですね、まだ　ヨーロッパを　りょ行した　ことが　ありませんから、今年は
いっか月ぐらい　ひとりで　ヨーロッパを　りょ行しようと　おもって　います。

たなか: ヨーロッパの　どこへ　行きますか。

すずき: イギリスや　フランスや　ドイツへ　行こうと　おもって　います。スペインへも

行こうと　おもって　います。できれば　ギリシャへも　行って　みたいです。たなかさんの

ほうふは　何ですか。

たなか: 今年は　ピアノを　ならおうと　おもって　います。

すずき: いいですね。どうしてですか。

たなか: むすめと　いっしょに　ピアノを　ひきたいんです。むすめは　ピアノを

3年ぐらい　ならって　います。それから、かぞくと　ふじ山に　のぼろうと

おもって　います。

すずき: そうですか。ところで　たなかさん、たばこを　やめた　ほうが　いいですよ。

たなか: はい、今年から　たばこを　やめようと　おもって　います。

1 すずきさんは　今年　何を　しようと　おもって　いますか。

_____

2 どうしてですか。

_____

3 たなかさんは　どうして　ピアノを　ならおうと　おもって　いますか。

_____

4 たなかさんは　かぞくと　何を　しようと　おもって　いますか。

_____

5 すずきさんは　たなかさんは　何を　した　ほうが　いいと　おもって　いますか。

_____

あけまして　おめでとう　ございます	_Happy New Year_
ほうふ	_(New Year's) resolution_
～か月	_months_
ぐらい	_about_
ひとりで	_by oneself_

The particle が

So far we have seen eight different uses for the particle が.

1 It is used with verbs of existence:

こうえんに　子どもが　います。　*There is a child in the park.*

2 It is used with adjectives describing people and places:

ロバートさんは　せが　高いです。　*Robert is tall.*

3 It is used with verbs and adjectives that take が marked objects:

たなかさんは　テニスが　上手です。　*Mr Tanaka is good at playing tennis.*

4 It is used in descriptions indicating *most*:

日本りょうりで　すしが　いちばん　おいしいです。　*Sushi is most delicious among Japanese dishes.*

5 It is used in descriptions of natural phenomenon:

雨が　ふって　います。　*It is raining.*

6 It is used in descriptions of ability.

ロバートさんは　かんじを　読む　ことが　できます。　*Robert can read kanji.*

7 It is used in descriptions of past experiences:

私は　ふじ山に　のぼった　ことが　あります。　*I have climbed Mt Fuji.*

8 It is used to express advice and make comparisons:

たばこを　やめた　ほうが　いいですよ。　*You had better give up smoking.*

I **Decide which meaning the particle が has and match the correct number from the examples above.**

1　たなかさんは　えい語が　分かります。(3)

2　エドワードさんは　おきなわへ　行った　ことが　ありません。( )

3　すずきさんは　かみが　長いです。( )

4　きのう　ゆきが　ふって　いました。( )

5　うちに　テレビが　2だい　あります。( )

6　スポーツで　サッカーが　いちばん　おもしろいです。( )

7　バスより　電車の　ほうが　はやいです。( )

8　ここで　本を　かりる　ことが　できます。( )

📝 Writing

J It is the end of the year and you have made your New Year's resolution: you have finally decided to visit Japan for a month! You intend to visit Tokyo and climb Mt Fuji. You are also thinking of visiting many places such as Kyoto, Osaka, Nara, etc. You would like to go to Hiroshima and Nagasaki too, if possible. Please list three other things that you intend to do while visiting Japan. Describe your resolution to your friends.

Japanese script

We will introduce four kanji in this unit.

Kanji	Reading	Meaning	Example words
一	いち、いっ、ひと(つ)、ひと(り)	*one*	^{いちがつ}一月、^{いっ}一^{げつ}か月、^{ついたち}一日 (*the first*)、 ^{いちにち}一日 (*a day*)、一人^{ひとり}
二	に、ふた(つ)、ふた(り)	*two*	^{に がつ}二月、^{ふつか}二日、^{に じ}二時、^{に ねん}二年、^{ふたり}二人
三	さん、みっ(つ)	*three*	^{さんがつ}三月、^{さんじ}三時、^{さん ねん}三年、^{さん にん}三人、 三つ^{みっ}
四	し、よん、よ、よっ(つ)	*four*	^{しがつ}四月、^{よ じ}四時、^{よにん}四人、^{よ ねん}四年、^{よにん}四人

K Choose the correct kanji to complete the sentences.

一 二人 三年間 四月 男 学校 木 語 好

1 _____、えい____を おしえた ことが あります。

2 スポーツで サッカーが____ばん____きです。

3 日本^{にほん}の_____は_____に はじまります。

4 ____の 下に^{した}____の子が^こ_____います。

Self-check

Tick the box which matches your level of confidence.

    1 = very confident   2 = need more practice   3 = not confident

下のボックスにじしんがあるかないかチェックしましょう。

    1. じしんがある   2. れんしゅうがひつよう   3. じしんがない

	1	2	3
Forming the plain volitional form.			
Expressing suggestions in plain style conversations.			
Expressing what the speaker is thinking of doing.			
Expressing trying to do something but failing to do so.			
Using the particle が.			
Recognizing the kanji for *one, two, three* and *four*.			

*For more information on the plain volitional form and how to express suggestions in plain style conversations, how to express what the speaker is thinking of doing, and how to express trying to do something but failing to do so refer to *Complete Japanese,* Unit 12.

17 この　へやに　はいらないで　ください。

Please do not enter this room.

CEFR: Can write very brief reports to a standard, conventionalized format, which pass on routine factual information and state reasons for actions (B1); Can read straightforward factual texts on subjects related to his field and interest with a satisfactory level of comprehension (B1).

Meaning and usage

The plain negative form is also called the ない form, and it has several uses. In this unit, we will look at four of them.

1 to express *not* in plain style conversations:

時間が　ないから　あさごはんを　食べない。　*I don't eat breakfast as I don't have time.*

きのう　うちへ　かえらなかった。　*I didn't go home yesterday.*

2 to ask or request someone not to do something, using ～ないで　ください:

この　へやに　入らないで　ください。*Please do not enter this room.*

ここで　ビールを　飲まないで　ください。
Please don't drink beer here.

3 to express doing something without something else, using ～ないで:

けいたいを　もたないで　出かけました。
I went out without my mobile phone.

Be sure to add で (not て) after ない. In order to express with, the て form is used.
けいたいを　もって　出かけました。
I went out with my mobile phone.

4 to express doing something instead of something else, using ～ないで:

車を　かわないで　ちょ金します。　*I won't buy a car, I will save money (I will save money instead of buying a car).*

Vocabulary

あるきます　I	*walk*
のります　I	*get on (transport)*
ぬれます　II	*be wet*
入れます　II	*put in*
かけます　II	*put on*
めがねを　かけます　II	*put glasses on*
しんぱいします　III	*worry*
ゆっくりします　III	*relax*
さとう	*sugar*
かさ	*umbrella*
としょかん	*library*

How to form the plain negative form (present and past)

Group I verbs

You need to change the last sound of the ます form stem from *i* to *a*, and add ない (present) or なかった (past), except:

1   when forming the plain negative of あります, it is simply ない (present) or なかった (past).

2   when forming the plain negative of verbs whose ます stem ends in い (such as かいます, あいます, つかいます) , then replace い with わ and add ない (present) or なかった (past).

A Complete the table.

ます form	Plain negative present	Plain negative past	English
かいます	かわない		*buy*
		つかわなかった	*use*
あいます			*meet*
	またない		*wait*
もちます			*hold, carry*
		入らなかった	*enter*
のります			*get on*
	飲まない		*drink*
休みます			*rest*

ます form	Plain negative present	Plain negative past	English
		えらばなかった	choose, select
	あそばない		play
あるきます			walk
		行かなかった	go
およぎます			swim
	いそがない		hurry
なくします			lose
		話さなかった	talk
あります			exist, have

B Complete the sentences by choosing the correct verbs from the box and changing them to the appropriate negative form, present or past.

> 読みます 分ります およぎます あります すいます もらいます 行きます

1 けさ　しんぶんを　読まなかった。
2 きょ年の　たんじょう日に　何も　_____。
3 あしたは　学校へ　_____。
4 きのう　ジムで　_____。
5 私は　一ども　日本へ　行った　ことが　_____。
6 この　かんじが　_____。
7 あしたから　たばこを　_____。

Group II verbs

You need to add ない after the ます form stem.

C Complete the table.

ます form	Plain negative present	Plain negative past	English
ねます			sleep
	食べない		eat
		わすれなかった	forget
	とめない		park, stop
出かけます			go out
	入れない		put in
かけます			put on (glasses)

			exist
います			exist
	<ruby>見<rt>み</rt></ruby>ない		look, watch
かります			borrow
		できなかった	be able to, can

Group III verbs

D Complete the table.

ます form	Plain negative present	Plain negative past	English
します	しない		do
		べんきょうしなかった	study
しんぱいします			worry
	ゆっくりしない		relax
<ruby>来<rt>き</rt></ruby>ます	<ruby>来<rt>こ</rt></ruby>ない		come

E Complete the sentences by choosing the correct verbs from the box and changing them to appropriate negative form, present or past.

> います <ruby>来<rt>き</rt></ruby>ます うんてんします できます <ruby>見<rt>み</rt></ruby>ます <ruby>食<rt>た</rt></ruby>べます

1 ロバートさんは　<ruby>先<rt>せん</rt></ruby>しゅう　パーティーへ _____

2 けさ　あさごはんを _____

3 きのう　テレビを _____

4 すずきさんは　けっこんして _____

5 ギターを　ひく　ことが _____

6 ビールを　<ruby>飲<rt>の</rt></ruby>んだ　<ruby>後<rt>あと</rt></ruby>は _____

F Translate the requests.

1 *Please do not use mobile phones here.*

　ここで　けいたいを　つかわないで　ください。

2 *Please do not talk in the library.*

_____

3 *Please do not lose (your) passport.*

_____

4 *Please do not forget (our) promise.*

_____

5 *Please do not park (your) car here.*

_____

6 *Please do not take pictures here.*

_____

7 *Please do not smoke here.*

_____

8 *Please do not worry.*

_____

G **Complete the sentences by changing the verbs in brackets into the negative form.**

1 私は　さとうを_____（入れます）で　コーヒーを　飲みます。

2 あさごはんを_____（食べます）で　かいしゃへ　行きました。

3 きのうの　ばん　かさを_____（もちます）で　出かけましたから、ぬれて　しまいました。

4 _____（いそぎます）で　ひるごはんを　食べます。

5 めがねを_____（かけます）で　本を　読みます。

6 今ばんは　ビールを_____（飲みます）で　うちへ　かえります。

H **Complete the sentences by choosing the correct verbs from the box and changing them to appropriate negative form.**

> かえります　のります　ねます　します　あそびます

1 今しゅうの　日よう日は　何も_____で　うちで　ゆっくりします。

2 きのうの　ばん、_____で　レポートを　書きました。

3 今年の　なつ休みは　イギリスへ_____で　日本を　りょ行します。

4 来しゅうは_____で　べんきょうします。

5 私は　いつも　バスに_____で　あるきます。

The plain forms for adjectives and nouns

In order to form the plain forms of い adjectives, simply remove です(see Unit 6). For the plain affirmative forms of な adjectives and nouns, simply replace です with だ (see Unit 5) and でした with だった. For the plain negative forms of な adjectives and nouns, simply remove です (Units 5 and 6).

I   Complete the table.

い adjectives

Affirmative present	Negative present	Affirmative past	Negative past
大^{おお}きい		大^{おお}きかった	
	高^{たか}くない		高^{たか}くなかった
いい		よかった	
	あつくない		あつくなかった

な adjectives

Affirmative present	Negative present	Affirmative past	Negative past
しずかだ		しずかだった	
	きれいじゃ　ない		きれいじゃ　なかった

Nouns

Affirmative present	Negative present	Affirmative past	Negative past
学生^{がくせい}だ		学生^{がくせい}だった	
	雨^{あめ}じゃ　ない		雨^{あめ}じゃ　なかった

Reading

J Read the blog by Miss Suzuki and answer the questions in Japanese.

Daily Blog

5月26日(金)

今日は　とても　いそがしかった。けさ、時間が　なかったから、
あさごはんを　食べないで　かいしゃへ　行ったが、いそいで
いたので、さいふを　わすれて　しまった。午前中は　メイルを
読んだり、電話を　かけたり　した。コーヒーを　3ばい　飲んだ。
12時から　3時まで　レポートを　書いた。それから、
ロバートさんに　お金を　かりて、やっと　ひるごはんを　食べた。
ひるごはんの　後で　2時間　かいぎが　あった。とても　長くて、
おもしろくなかった。

しごとが　おわった　後で、　ロバートさんと　たなかさんと
飲みに　行った。　そして、　10時ごろまで　カラオケを　して、
12時ごろ　うちへ　かえった。　たのしかったが、　とても
つかれた。　あしたは　何も　しないで、　うちで　ゆっくりしよう。

---

1 すずきさんは　どうして　けさ　あさごはんを　食べませんでしたか。

_____

2 午前中に　何を　しましたか。

_____

3 何時に　ひるごはんを　食べましたか。

_____

4 どうして　ロバートさんに　お金を　かりましたか。

_____

5 かいぎは　どうでしたか。

_____

6 しごとの　後で　何を　しましたか。

_____

7 あした　何を　しようと　おもって　いますか。

_____

午前中 <small>ごぜんちゅう</small>	_in the morning_
〜ばい	_〜 cups (counter for cups)_
やっと	_at last_
〜時ごろ <small>じ</small>	_around 〜 o'clock_

📝 Writing

K Describe a busy day in the plain form. You didn't have enough time in the morning so you went to work without having breakfast. You didn't eat lunch until 3 p.m. You worked till 7 p.m., reading and writing emails and making phone calls. You went to see a film with your friends after work, but it was long and boring. You then went to a restaurant to have dinner. The dinner wasn't delicious! You decided you are going to the gym tomorrow after work to swim instead of going for a drink.

Japanese script

We will introduce four kanji in this unit.

Kanji	Reading	Meaning	Example words
五	ご、いつ(つ)	*five*	<ruby>五月<rt>ごがつ</rt></ruby>、<ruby>五日<rt>いつか</rt></ruby>、<ruby>五<rt>いつ</rt></ruby>つ、 <ruby>五人<rt>ごにん</rt></ruby>、 <ruby>五本<rt>ごほん</rt></ruby>
六	ろく、ろっ, むっ(つ)、むい(か)	*six*	<ruby>六月<rt>ろくがつ</rt></ruby>、<ruby>六日<rt>むいか</rt></ruby>、<ruby>六<rt>むっ</rt></ruby>つ、 <ruby>六人<rt>ろくにん</rt></ruby>、 <ruby>六本<rt>ろっぽん</rt></ruby>
七	しち、なな、 なな(つ)、なの(か)	*seven*	<ruby>七月<rt>しちがつ</rt></ruby>、<ruby>七時<rt>しちじ</rt></ruby>、<ruby>七<rt>なな</rt></ruby>つ、 <ruby>七日<rt>なのか</rt></ruby>、<ruby>七本<rt>ななほん</rt></ruby>
八	はち、はっ, やっ(つ)、よう(か)	*eight*	<ruby>八月<rt>はちがつ</rt></ruby>、<ruby>八日<rt>ようか</rt></ruby>、<ruby>八<rt>やっ</rt></ruby>つ、 <ruby>八本<rt>はっぽん</rt></ruby>、<ruby>八時<rt>はちじ</rt></ruby>

L   Choose the correct kanji to complete the sentences.

七本　子　日本　毎日　八月　六時　五月五日

1 ＿＿＿＿＿＿＿ は、＿＿＿＿＿＿＿ どもの　<ruby>日<rt>ひ</rt></ruby>です。

2 ＿＿＿＿＿＿＿ 、＿＿＿＿＿＿＿ まで　はたらきます。

3 ビールを＿＿＿＿＿＿＿＿ かいました。

4 ＿＿＿＿＿＿＿ の＿＿＿＿＿＿＿ は　あついです。

Self-check

Tick the box which matches your level of confidence.

1 = very confident   2 = need more practice   3 = not confident

下のボックスにじしんがあるかないかチェックしましょう。

1. じしんがある   2. れんしゅうがひつよう   3. じしんがない

	1	2	3
Forming plain negative forms.			
Asking or requesting someone not to do something.			
Saying *without doing*.			
Expressing doing something instead of something else.			
Forming the plain forms for adjectives and nouns.			
Recognizing the kanji for *five*, *six*, *seven* and *eight*.			

*For more information on the plain negative form and how to ask or request someone not to do something, how to say *without doing* and how to form the plain forms for adjectives and nouns refer to *Complete Japanese,* Unit 13.

18 あした　あめが　ふるかも　しれません。

It might possibly rain tomorrow.

In this unit you will learn to:

✓ Express varying probability and possibility using the plain form.

✓ Express *I decided*.

✓ Express decisions and arrangements that the speaker is not solely in control of making.

✓ Express how things are supposed to be as a rule or custom.

✓ Use the particle が when the topic is not the subject of the sentence.

✓ Recognize the kanji for *nine, ten, hundred* and *thousand*.

CEFR: Can summarize, report and give opinion about accumulated factual information on familiar matters with some confidence (B1); Can briefly give reasons and explanations for opinions and plans, and actions (B1); Can summarize and give opinion of material (B1).

Meaning and usage

The plain forms, both affirmative and negative, are used to express varying degrees of certainty and probability.

1 to express that the speaker has grounds to believe something to be true, using 〜はずです:

たなかさんは　イギリスに　二年間（にねんかん）　すんでいましたから、えい語（ご）が
分（わ）かる　はずです。　　*Mr Tanaka should be able to understand English as he has lived in the UK for two years.*

Here the speaker makes a judgement that Mr Tanaka should be able to understand English based on the fact that he has lived in the UK for two years.

2 to express that something will probably happen, using 〜でしょう:

あした　雨（あめ）が　ふるでしょう。　　*It will probably rain tomorrow.*

あした　雨（あめ）が　ふらないでしょう。　　*It will probably not rain tomorrow.*

3 to express that there is a chance something might possibly happen, using 〜かも　しれません:

あした　雨（あめ）が　ふるかも　しれません。
It might possibly rain tomorrow.

 These examples are in order of certainty with 〜はずです being the most certain.

4 to express tentatively that something might happen, using 〜んじゃ　ないでしょうか. This form is used to express politeness or to show someone respect as well:

やまだ先生は　あした　<u>休む</u>んじゃ　ないでしょうか。
Is it at all possible that Mr Yamada will take a day off tomorrow?

Vocabulary

おくります　Ⅰ		*send*
つきます　Ⅰ		*arrive*
たります　Ⅱ		*be enough*
はれます　Ⅱ		*clear up*
間に　あいます　Ⅰ		*be in time*
しゅっせきします　Ⅲ		*attend*
あらいます　Ⅰ		*wash*
ぬぎます　Ⅰ		*take off (clothing)*
にもつ		*baggage, parcel*
そうべつかい		*farewell party*
からだ		*body*
〜がわ		*〜side*
べつべつに		*separately*
エスカレーター		*escalator*

A **Complete the sentences by choosing the correct verbs from the box and changing them to the appropriate forms.**

> おしえました　できます　つきます　食べません　読みます　しって　います
> やくそくしました　分かります　来ます　おくりました

1 きのう ＿＿＿＿＿＿＿のので、たなかさんは　パーティーへ ＿＿＿＿＿＿＿ はずです。

2 ロバートさんは　日本語を　べんきょうして　いますから、かんじを ＿＿＿＿＿＿＿こと
　が ＿＿＿＿＿＿＿ はずです。

3 やまだ先生は　ドイツで　日本語を ＿＿＿＿＿＿＿ことが　ありますから、
　ドイツ語が ＿＿＿＿＿＿＿ はずです。

4 今日　にもつを ＿＿＿＿＿＿＿のので、水ようび日に ＿＿＿＿＿＿＿ はずです。

5 ロバートさんは　たなかさんの　友だちですから、たなかさんを　よく ＿＿＿＿＿＿＿
　はずです。

6 エドワードさんは　ベジタリアンですから、にくを ＿＿＿＿＿＿＿ はずです。

B Complete the sentences by changing the words in brackets into the appropriate forms.

1 これから _____ (さむいです) く _____ (なります) でしょう。

2 あしたは _____ (はれます) でしょう。

3 すずきさんは 今日 しごとが _____ (あります) ので、パーティーへ _____ (来ません) でしょう。

4 日本で _____ (やすいです) て いい ラップトップを _____ (かいます) ことが _____ (できます) でしょう。

5 やまだ先生は おさけが あまり 好きじゃ ないですから、今ばん _____ (飲みません) でしょう。

6 11時ですから、たなかさんは _____ (ねて います) でしょう。

C Complete the sentences by changing the words in brackets into the appropriate forms.

1 あたまが _____ (いたいです) ので、あした かいしゃを _____ (休みます) かも しれません。

2 あした ゆきが _____ (ふります) かも しれません。

3 しごとが _____ (つまらないです) ので、かいしゃを _____ (やめます) かも しれません。

4 すみません、今日の レッスンに _____ (しゅっせきします) ことが _____ (できません) かも しれません。

5 やくそくの 時間に _____ (間に あいません) かも しれませんから、いそぎましょう。

6 たなかさんは 時間が _____ あります) ので、今日の パーティーに _____ (来ます) かも しれません。

D Complete the sentences by choosing the correct verbs from the box and changing them to the appropriate forms.

> あります かいます のぼりました 食べます しんぱいして います たりません はたらきません

1 エドワードさんは ベジタリアンですが、さかなを _____ んじゃ ないでしょうか。

2 お金が _____ んじゃ ないでしょうか。

3 ロバートさんは しんじゅくで あたらしい けいたいを _____ んじゃ ないでしょうか。

4 やまだ先生は あした _____ んじゃ ないでしょうか。

5 たなかさんは 前に ふじ山に _____ ことが _____ んじゃ ないでしょうか。

6 お父さんと お母さんは _____ んじゃ ないでしょうか。

Meaning and usage: more on the plain form

The plain form is also used to express decisions, things you do as a rule or habit, arrangements and customs.

1 to express *I decided*, using 〜ことに　しました:

かいしゃを　やめる　ことに　しました。　　　*I decided to quit the job.*

2 to express things you do as a rule or habit, using the progressive form 〜ことに
して　います:

毎しゅう　ジムへ　行く　ことに　して　います。 *As a rule I go to the gym every week (I make a point of going to the gym every week).*

3 to express decisions and arrangements that the speaker is not solely in control of making, using
〜ことに　なりました:

ITの　かいしゃで　はたらく　ことに　なりました。
It has been arranged that I will work for an IT company (I shall be working for an IT company).

来年　けっこんする　ことに　なりました。
It has been decided that I will get married next year (we have decided to get married next year).

 This expression is often used even if you decide to marry, or to accept a job, as Japanese people tend to want to appear more humble and less boastful.

4 to express how things are supposed to be as a rule or custom, using the progressive form 〜ことに
なって　います:

日本では、うちに　入る　前に　くつを　ぬぐ　ことに　なって　います。　*You are supposed to take off your shoes before entering a house in Japan (It is a custom in Japan to take off your shoes when entering a house).*

E　Transform the sentences into sentences that express a decision or rule.

1 今日から　たばこを　やめます。
今日から　たばこを　やめる　ことに　しました。

2 毎しゅう　ブログを　書いて　います。
毎しゅう　ブログを　書く　ことに　して　います。

3 今年の　なつ休みに　ヨーロッパを　りょ行します。

_____

4 毎日　やさいを　食べて　います。

_____

5 来月　国へ　かえります。

_____

6 いつも　バスに　のらないで、あるいて　います。

_____

7 べつべつに　はらいましょう。

_____

F Complete the sentences by changing the verbs in brackets into the plain form. Also, decide whether the sentences express arrangements or customs by choosing either なりました **or** なっています.

1 来しゅうの　金よう日に　エドワードさんの　そうべつかいを　する（します）ことに　（なりました／~~なっています~~）。

2 来月から　大学で　日本語を_____（おしえます）ことに　（なりました／なって　います）。

3 日本では　おふろに_____（入ります）　前に　からだを_____（あらいます）ことに　（なりました／なって　います）。

4 イギリスでは　エスカレーターの　右がわに_____（たちます）ことに　（なりました／なって　います）。

5 大さかに_____（すみます）ことに　（なりました／なって　います）。

6 日本と　イギリスでは　みちの　左がわを_____（うんてんします）ことに　（なりました／なって　います）。

 # Reading

G **Read the email from Edward to Miss Suzuki, and answer the questions in Japanese.**

From:	
To:	
Subject:	

すずきさん、

こんにちは。おげんきですか。

私は　今月　かいしゃを　やめて、来月から　大さかで　はたらく　ことに
なりました。　今月の　22日に　ひっこしします。　ひっこしは　ロバートさんと
たなかさんが　てつだいに　来て　くれます。

あたらしい　しごとが　はじまる　前に、すこし　時間が　ありますから、
一しゅう間ぐらい　りょ行しようと　おもって　います。おきなわに　行った
ことが　ありませんから、行って　みたいです。おきなわには　友だちの
ほんださんが　すんで　いますから、あう　ことが　できるかも　しれません。

すずきさんは　今しゅうの　金よう日　ひまですか。たなかさんと
ロバートさんが　私の　そうべつかいを　ひらいて　くれます。できれば
来て　ください。

エドワード

1 エドワードさんは 何を する ことに なりましたか。

_____

2 いつ ひっこししますか。

_____

3 だれが てつだって くれますか。

_____

4 あたらしい しごとが はじまる 前に 何を しようと おもって いますか。

_____

5 今しゅうの 金よう日に 何が ありますか。

_____

～ぐらい	*about*
～を ひらきます I	*give (a party)*

The subject marker が

Did you notice that there are three instances of the particle が marking the subjects in the reading text?

1 ひっこしは ロバートさんと たなかさんが てつだいに 来て くれます。

2 おきなわには 友だちの ほんださんが すんでいます。

3 たなかさんと ロバートさんが 私の そうべつかいを ひらいて くれます。

Notice also in 1 and 2 above, the subjects of the sentences are preceded by topics. In fact, the topic of 3 is *Friday* from the preceding sentence, so 3 also has a topic that is not the subject of the sentence. The speaker assumes that the topics are already known to the listener. When the topic of a sentence is *not* also the subject of the sentence, the topic is marked with the topic marker は and then the subject is introduced with が. This is similar to the pattern we studied in Unit 5 with adjectives, such as ロバートさんは せが 高いです (*Robert is tall*). Also, when you want to ask *who did something*, the question word だれ is marked with が, as in Question 3 above. Compare the following sentences.

ロバートさんは この ケーキを つくりました。
(Robert is both the subject and the topic)

この　ケーキは　ロバートさんが　つくりました。
(*This cake* is the topic and Robert is the subject)

だれが　この　ケーキを　つくりましたか。

たなかさんは　この　レポートを　書きました。
(Mr Tanaka is both the subject and the topic)

このレポートは　たなかさんが　書きました。
(*This report* is the topic and Mr Tanaka is the subject)

だれが　この　レポートを　書きましたか。

H **Turn the objects of the following sentences into the topics, and mark the subjects with** が**.**

1 たなかさんは　この　とけいを　かって　くれました。
このとけいは　たなかさんが　かって　くれました。

2 ロバートさんは　この　メイルを　書きました。

_____

3 エドワードさんは　この　しゃしんを　とりました。

_____

4 私は　この　しごとを　やります。

_____

5 すずきさんは　この　えを　かきました。

_____

 Writing

I **Write an email to your friend Keiko. Inform her 1) that you are quitting your current job and starting a new one in Kyoto, 2) that you have some time before you start your new job so you are thinking of doing such things as going travelling and climbing Mt Fuji, 3) that it may be possible to meet your friend Mr Yamakawa as he lives near Mt Fuji. End the email by 4) inviting her to your farewell party on Sunday this week that is being organized by your friends.**

From:	
To:	
Subject:	

Japanese script

We will introduce the four kanji in this unit.

Kanji	Reading	Meaning	Example words				
九	きゅう、く、ここの（つ）	nine	くがつ 九月、	くじ 九時、	ここのか 九日、	ここの 九つ、	きゅうほん 九本
十	じゅう、じゅっ、とお	ten	じゅうがつ 十月、	じゅっぷん 十分、	じゅうにん 十人、	とおか 十日	じゅうじ 十時
百	ひゃく、びゃく、ぴゃく	hundred	ひゃくえん 百円、	さんびゃく 三百、	はっぴゃく 八百		
千	せん、ぜん、ち	thousand	せん えん さん ぜん はっせん 千円、三千、八千				

J Choose the correct kanji to complete the sentences.

十二月二十五日	本	三百六十五日	毎日	二十本	二千十二年	九百円

1 _____ たばこを _____ ぐらい　すいます。

2 _____ に　ロンドンで　オリンピックが　ありました。

3 この _____ は _____ です。

4 _____ は　クリスマスです。

いちねん
5 一年は _____ です。

Self-check

Tick the box which matches your level of confidence.

1 = very confident　　　2 = need more practice　　　3 = not confident

下のボックスにじしんがあるかないかチェックしましょう。

1. じしんがある　　　2. れんしゅうがひつよう　　　3. じしんがない

	1	2	3
Expressing varying probability and possibility using the plain form.			
Expressing *I decided*.			
Expressing things you do as a rule or habit.			
Expressing decisions and arrangements that the speaker is not solely in control of making.			
Expressing how things are supposed to be as a rule or custom.			
Using the particle が when the topic is not the subject of the sentence.			
Recognizing the kanji for *nine, ten, hundred* and *thousand*.			

*For more information on how to express degree of probabilities, how to say *I decided*, how to express things you do as a rule or habit, how to express decisions and arrangements that the speaker is not solely in control of making and how to express how things are supposed to be as a rule or custom refer to *Complete Japanese,* Unit 12.

19 にちようびは　はたらかなくても　いいです。

I don't have to work on Sunday.

In this unit you will learn to:

- ✓ Express obligation.
- ✓ Express not having to do something.
- ✓ Give advice against doing something.
- ✓ Express two actions taking place throughout a time period.
- ✓ Express two actions taking place at some point in time.
- ✓ Express an action taking place before something else occurs.
- ✓ Use particles.
- ✓ Recognize the kanji for *ten thousand, half, days of week* and *week*.

CEFR: Can write very brief reports to a standard, conventionalized format, which pass on routine factual information and state reasons for actions (B1); Can scan longer text in order to locate desired information in everyday material, such as letters, brochures and short official documents (B1); Can develop an argument well enough to be followed without difficulty most of the time; Can explain why something is a problem (B1).

Meaning and usage

In this unit, we will practise how to express obligation, not having to do something and giving advice by using the negative ない form.

1   to express obligation:

あした　午後　8時まで　はたらかなければ　なりません。
I have to work till 8 p.m. tomorrow.

毎日　午前　6時はんに　おきなければ　なりません。
I must get up at 6.30 a.m. every day.

In order to express obligation, you need to remove ない from the ない form and add the phrase なければ　なりません. It is a double negative construction, roughly meaning *it is no good if I/you/ they don't*. The plain form of なりません is ならない.

あしたも　しごとを　しなければ　ならない。
I must work tomorrow as well.

You saw how to express prohibition in Unit 9, using ては　いけません.
Compare the meaning between obligation and prohibition:

コンピューターを　つかっては　いけません。
You must not *use a computer.*

コンピューターを　つかわなければ　なりません。
You must use a computer.

2   to express not having to do something:
<ruby>日<rt>にち</rt></ruby>よう<ruby>日<rt>び</rt></ruby>は　はたらかなくても　いいです。
I don't have to work on Sunday.
<ruby>日<rt>にち</rt></ruby>よう<ruby>日<rt>び</rt></ruby>は　はやく　おきなくても　いいです。
I don't have to get up early on Sunday.

Remember the character は *in* 日よう日は *is the topic marker so it is pronounced 'wa' while* は *in* はたらかなくても *is pronounced 'ha'.*

You have in fact seen a very similar structure in Unit 9, when asking for and granting permission. To express *not having to something*, you need to remove ない from the ない form and add the phrase なくても　いいです. As discussed in Unit 9, this structure is a conditional form, meaning *it is OK even if I/you/they don't.* Compare:

コンピューターを　つかっても　いいです。　*You may use a computer.*

コンピューターを　つかわなくても　いいです。*You don't have to use a computer.*

3   to give advice against doing something, using ない form plus ほうが　いいです:

しごとを　やめない　ほうが　いいです。　　*You should not quit your job.*

You saw a similar structure in Unit 15, using the た form plus ほうが　いいです. Compare:

コンピューターを　つかった　ほうが　いいです。　*You should use a computer.*

コンピューターを　つかわない　ほうが　いいです。　*You should not use a computer.*

Vocabulary

かいものします　Ⅲ	*shop (literally, to do shopping)*
さめます　Ⅱ	*get cold (temperature)*
かぜ	*cold (illness)*
かぜを　ひきます　Ⅰ	*catch a cold*
レッスン	*lesson*
いえ	*house*
くうこう	*airport*
しょくじ	*meal*
しゅうまつ	*weekend*
ねむい	*sleepy*
おそく	*late*

A Complete the sentences by changing the verbs in brackets.

1 あした　びょういんへ＿＿＿＿＿＿＿（行きます）ば　なりません。

2 ねる　前に　この　くすりを＿＿＿＿＿＿＿（飲みます）ば　なりません。

3 毎しゅう　15まい　レポートを＿＿＿＿＿＿＿（書きます）ば
なりません。

4 日本語の　レッスンでは　いつも　日本語で＿＿＿＿＿＿＿（話します）ば
なりません。

5 くうこうで　パスポートを＿＿＿＿＿＿＿（見せます）ば　なりません。

6 日本人の　いえに　入る　とき、くつを＿＿＿＿＿＿＿（ぬぎます）ば
なりません。

B Complete the sentences by changing the verbs in brackets.

1 しゅうまつは　はやく　<u>おきなくて</u>（おきます）も　いいです。

2 今日の　かいぎに＿＿＿＿＿＿＿（しゅっせきします）も　いいです。

3 時間が　ありますから、＿＿＿＿＿＿＿（いそぎます）も　いいです。

4 あした　かいしゃへ＿＿＿＿＿＿＿（行きます）も　いいです。

5 今ばん　しょくじを＿＿＿＿＿＿＿（つくります）も　いいです。

6 この　レストランは　げん金で＿＿＿＿＿＿＿（はらいます）も　いいです。

7 あしたの　パーティーへ＿＿＿＿＿＿＿（来ます）も　いいです。

C Complete the advice sentences by choosing the correct verbs from the box and changing them into appropriate forms – it could be the た or the ない form.

> 休みます　かけます　見ます　飲みます　やめます　うんてんします
> れんらくします

1 毎ばん、おさけを＿＿＿＿＿＿＿ほうが　いいです。

2 ねむい　とき、＿＿＿＿＿＿＿ほうが　いいです。

3 ねつが　ある　とき、かいしゃを＿＿＿＿＿＿＿ほうが　いいです。

4 たばこを＿＿＿＿＿＿＿ほうが　いいです。

5 11時ですから、電話を＿＿＿＿＿＿＿ほうが　いいです。

6 かぜを　ひいた　ときは、学校に＿＿＿＿＿＿＿ほうが　いいです。

7 おそくまで　テレビを＿＿＿＿＿＿＿ほうが　いいです。

How to express more than two actions occurring simultaneously

In Unit 7, we learnt to express one person doing two actions simultaneously, using ～ながら.

まいあさ、コーヒーを　飲<ruby>の</ruby>みながら、しんぶんを　読<ruby>よ</ruby>みます。

Every morning, I read the newspaper while drinking coffee.

In order to express two actions by one or more people, but which are taking place at the same time, you need to use ～間<ruby>あいだ</ruby>, ～間<ruby>あいだ</ruby>に or ～うちに.

1 to express two actions by two people taking place during the time specified by the clause containing 間<ruby>あいだ</ruby>:

1.1　たなかさんが　電話<ruby>でんわ</ruby>を　かけて　いる　間<ruby>あいだ</ruby>、すずきさんは　レポートを　書<ruby>か</ruby>きました。　*Miss Suzuki wrote a report while Mr Tanaka made a phone call.*

It is important to note that Miss Suzuki was writing a report *throughout* the time Mr Tanaka was on the phone. Note also that the subject of the clause containing 間<ruby>あいだ</ruby>(たなかさん) is marked with the subject marker が. When the subject of the actions are the same, then it is marked with the topic marker は.

1.2　私<ruby>わたし</ruby>は　イギリスに　いる　間<ruby>あいだ</ruby>、えい語<ruby>ご</ruby>を　べんきょうしました。
I was studying English throughout the time I was in the UK.

2 to express two actions by two people taking place at some point within the time specified by the clause containing 間<ruby>あいだ</ruby>に:

2.1　たなかさんが　電話<ruby>でんわ</ruby>を　かけて　いる　間<ruby>あいだ</ruby>に、すずきさんは　レポートを　書<ruby>か</ruby>きました。　*Miss Suzuki wrote the report (and finished it) while Mr Tanaka made a phone call.*

In 2.1, Miss Suzuki wrote the report at some point during the time Mr Tanaka was on the phone, which implies she finished writing it during that time also.

2.2　私<ruby>わたし</ruby>は　イギリスに　いる　間<ruby>あいだ</ruby>に、友<ruby>とも</ruby>だちに　あいました。
I saw my friend while I was in the UK.

3 to express *while it is not* or *before something occurs*, using ない form plus うちに:

3.1　子<ruby>こ</ruby>どもが　おきない　うちに　しょくじを つくります。　*I cook before the children wake up / I cook while they are not awake.*

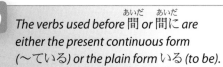

The verbs used before 間<ruby>あいだ</ruby> or 間<ruby>あいだ</ruby>に are either the present continuous form (～ている) or the plain form いる (to be).

This form is often used when the speaker doesn't know exactly when something happens. For example, in 3.1, the speaker is unsure exactly when the children will wake up.

D Complete the sentences by changing the verbs in brackets.

1 すずきさんが＿＿＿＿＿＿＿＿（かいものします）間、ロバートさんは
コーヒーを　飲みました。

2 エドワードさんが　本を＿＿＿＿＿＿＿（読みます）間、ロバートさんは
おんがくを　聞いていました。

3 ロバートさんが　しごとを＿＿＿＿＿＿（します）間、たなかさんは　えいがを　見ました。

4 子どもが　学校へ＿＿＿＿＿＿（行きます）間、私は　そうじしたり、せんたくしたり　します。

5 すずきさんと　ロバートさんが＿＿＿＿＿＿（話します）間、たなかさんは
レポートを　書きました。

E Complete the sentences by changing the verbs in brackets.

1 かぞくが＿＿＿＿＿＿（ねます）間に　うちを　出ました。

2 えいがを＿＿＿＿＿＿（見ます）間に　ねて　しまいました。

3 子どもが＿＿＿＿＿＿（べんきょうします）間に　かいものを　しました。

4 日本に＿＿＿＿＿＿（います）間に　ふじ山に　のぼって　みたいです。

5 たなかさんが　おふろに＿＿＿＿＿＿（入ります）間に　おくさんは
しょくじを　つくりました。

F Complete the sentences by choosing the correct verbs from the box and changing them into the negative form.

わすれます　はじまります　さめます　ふります　来ます

1 雨が＿＿＿＿＿＿うちに　出かけましょう。

2 ＿＿＿＿＿＿うちに　電話を　かけます。

3 友だちが＿＿＿＿＿＿うちに　へやを　そうじします。

4 えいがが＿＿＿＿＿＿うちに　トイレへ　行きます。

5 どうぞ、コーヒーです。＿＿＿＿＿＿うちに　飲んで　ください。

G Complete the sentences by choosing the correct particles.
Is it は, が, を, に, へ, で, の **or** と**?**

1 たなかさん＿＿＿えい語＿＿＿分かる　はずです。

2 私＿＿＿日本語＿＿＿話す　こと＿＿＿できます。

3 この　ケーキ____ロバートさん____つくりました。

4 友だち____レストラン____ばんごはん____食べました。

5 ロバートさん____せ____高いです。

6 うち____テレビ____2だい　あります。

7 母___日___母___　白い　はな___あげました。

8 ロバートさん____おんがく____聞いている　間、すずきさん____

　たなかさん___本___読みました。

9 今日、びじゅつかん___え___見___行きます。

📖 Reading

H **Read the following text about Robert's business trip to Osaka and answer the questions in Japanese.**

	ロバートさんは　あしたから　二日間、しごとで　大さかへ　行く　ことに　なりました。
	午前　7時の　しんかんせんに　のる　よていですから、あしたは　午前　5時はんに
	おきなければ　なりません。とうきょうえきから　大さかえきまで　3時間ぐらい　かかります。
	10時に　大さかししゃの　たにぐちさんと　話して、それから、ひるごはんを　食べます。
	そして、1時から　かいぎに　しゅっせきしなければ　なりません。ロバートさんは　かいぎで
	あたらしい　コンピューターソフトの　はっぴょうを　します。日本語で　はっぴょうを
	しなければ　なりませんから、ロバートさんは　きんちょうして　います。かいぎの　後で
	レポートを　書かなければ　なりません。あしたの　ばんは　大さかホテルに　とまります。
	あさっては、午前　9時から　11時まで　また　かいぎが　ありますが、午後は　何も　しなくても
	いいですから、ロバートさんは　大さかじょうへ　行こうと　おもって　います。それから、
	エドワードさんに　あって、ばんごはんを　いっしょに　食べて、8時の　しんかんせんで
	とうきょうへ　かえります。

1 ロバートさんは　あしたから　何_{なに}を　する　ことに　なりましたか。

_____

2 あした　何時_{なんじ}に　おきなければ　なりませんか。

_____

3 どうしてですか。

_____

4 あしたの　1時_じから　何_{なに}を　しなければ　なりませんか。

_____

5 ロバートさんは　どうして　きんちょうして　いますか。

_____

6 ロバートさんは　あさって、どこへ　行_いこうと　おもって　いますか。

_____

7 どうしてですか。

_____

かかります　I		_take_
ししゃ		_branch office_
はっぴょう		_presentation_
きんちょうします　III		_be nervous_
とまります　I		_stay_
あさって		_the day after tomorrow_
大_{おお}さかじょう		_Osaka castle_

 # Writing

I   It has been arranged that you are to go on a business trip to Kyoto tomorrow. Describe
what you must do and don't have to do. You must 1) get up at 5.00 a.m. to catch the 6.30
a.m. Shinkansen (しんかんせん), 2) meet and talk to Mr Tanaka for about an hour, 3) attend
a meeting from 2 p.m., 4) give a presentation at the meeting on a new product (せいひん) in
Japanese. The meeting ends at 4 p.m. and you do not have to do anything after the meeting, so
you are thinking of visiting Kiyomizu temple (きよみずでら) with your friend Anne. You plan to
get on the 8 p.m. Shinkansen back to Tokyo.

Japanese script

We will introduce four kanji in this unit.

KANJI	READING	MEANING	EXAMPLE WORDS
万	まん、ばん	*ten thousand*	<ruby>一万円<rt>いちまんえん</rt></ruby>、 <ruby>百万<rt>ひゃくまん</rt></ruby> *(one million)*
半	はん, なか(ば)	*half*	<ruby>半分<rt>はんぶん</rt></ruby> *(half)*、 5<ruby>時半<rt>じはん</rt></ruby>
曜	よう	*day of the week*	<ruby>月曜日<rt>げつようび</rt></ruby>、 <ruby>水曜日<rt>すいようび</rt></ruby>
週	しゅう	*week*	<ruby>毎週<rt>まいしゅう</rt></ruby>、 <ruby>今週<rt>こんしゅう</rt></ruby>、 <ruby>来週<rt>らいしゅう</rt></ruby>

J Choose the correct kanji to complete the sentences.

日本語　　毎週　　百万円　　書　　毎　　時半　　車　　火曜日　　行

1 この＿＿＿＿＿＿は＿＿＿＿＿＿です。

2 ＿＿＿＿＿＿あさ、6＿＿＿＿＿＿に　おきなければ　なりません。

3 ロバートさんは＿＿＿＿＿＿に＿＿＿＿＿＿の　レッスンへ＿＿＿＿＿＿きます。

4 たなかさんは＿＿＿＿＿＿レポートを＿＿＿＿＿＿きます。

Self-check

Tick the box which matches your level of confidence.

1 = very confident   2 = need more practice   3 = not confident

下のボックスにじしんがあるかないかチェックしましょう。

1. じしんがある   2. れんしゅうがひつよう   3. じしんがない

	1	2	3
Expressing obligation.			
Expressing not having to do something.			
Giving advice against doing something.			
Expressing two actions taking place throughout a time period.			
Expressing two actions taking place at some point in time.			
Expressing an action taking place before something else occurs.			
Using particles.			
Recognizing the kanji for *ten thousand, half, days of week* and *week*.			

*For more information on how to express obligation and not having to something, how to give advice against doing something, how to express two actions taking place throughout a time period, how to express two actions taking place at some point in time and how to express an action taking place before something else occurs refer to *Complete Japanese*, Unit 13.

20 おかねと　じかんが　あったら　りょこうします。

I will travel if I have money and time.

In this unit you will learn to:

- ✓ Express *if*, *when*, and *even if* using verbs.
- ✓ Express *if* and *even if* using adjectives and nouns.
- ✓ Recognize the kanji for *mouth*, *north*, *south*, *east* and *west*.

CEFR: Can summarize, report and give opinion about accumulated factual information on familiar matters with some confidence (B1); Can identify the main conclusions in clearly signaled argumentative texts; Can recognize the line of argument in the treatment of the issue presented, but not necessarily in detail (B1).

Meaning and usage

In this unit, we will practise how to form the conditional forms. We can use these forms in the following ways.

1 to express *if*:

(もし)　お金と　時間が　<u>あったら</u>、りょ行します。　*I will travel if I have money and time.*

(もし)　お金が　<u>なかったら</u>、どこも　行きません。　*If I don't have money, then I won't go anywhere.*

The conditional *if* is expressed by using the past tense of the plain form (affirmative and negative) plus ら. もし (meaning *if*) is optional.

2 to express *when/after/once*:

10時に　<u>なったら</u>、かいぎを　はじめましょう。　*Let's start the meeting once it gets to ten.*

The clause containing the past tense of the plain form plus ら can also mean *when* if the situation described in that clause is sure to happen in future. In the above case, we are sure it will get to 10 o'clock at some point every day!

3 to express *even if/even though*:

お金と　時間が　<u>あっても</u>、りょ行しません。
I will not travel even if I had money and time.

お金が　<u>なくても</u>、出かけます。　*I will go out even if I don't have money.*

> 🍎 When もし *is used at the beginning of a sentence, then it is clearly a conditional sentence.*

The conditional *even if* is expressed by using the て form plus も. For the negative form, 〜なくても is used. We have already come across this form in expressing permission. Compare:

おさけを　<u>飲んでも</u>　いいです。　*You may drink alcohol/it is OK even if you drink alcohol.*

おさけを　<u>飲まなくても</u>　いいです。　*You don't have to drink alcohol. (Literally, 'it is OK even if you don't drink alcohol.')*

おさけを　<u>飲んでも</u>、たのしくないです。　*Even if I drink alcohol, it's not fun.*

おさけを　<u>飲まなく</u>ても、たのしいです。　*Even if I don't drink alcohol, it's fun.*

Vocabulary

こと	*thing*
日本の　こと	*(things) about Japan*
すぐ	*immediately*
つごう	*convenience*
つごうが　わるい	*inconvenient (concerning time)*
つづけます　II	*continue*
れんしゅうします　III	*practise*
ふべん(な)	*inconvenient*
むり(な)	*impossible*
1わりびき	*10 per cent off*

A　Complete the sentences by changing the verbs in brackets to express *if*.

1 あさ、時間が_____（ありません）ら、あさごはんを　食べません。

2 もし　時間が_____（あります）ら、えいがを　見ませんか。

3 雨が_____（ふります）ら、出かけません。

4 もし　休みを　一週間_____（もらいます）ら、日本へ　行きたいです。

5 タクシーに_____（のります）ら、10時の　しんかんせんに
間に　あいます。

6 かぜを_____（ひきます）ら、学校を　休みます。

B Complete the sentences by changing the verbs in brackets to express *when/once/after.*

1 うちへ ＿＿＿＿＿ （かえります）ら、おふろに　入ります。

2 おさけを ＿＿＿＿＿（飲みます）ら、うんてんしません。

3 大学を ＿＿＿＿＿（出ます）ら、父の　かいしゃで　はたらきます。

4 60さいに ＿＿＿＿＿（なります）ら、しごとを　やめて、おきなわに　すみたいです。

5 かいぎが ＿＿＿＿＿（おわります）ら、ひるごはんを　食べましょう。

6 えきに ＿＿＿＿＿（つきます）ら、電話して　ください。

C Complete the sentences by changing the verbs in brackets into the appropriate form.

1 雨が ＿＿＿＿＿（ふります）も、出かけます。

2 つまらない　本を　＿＿＿＿＿（読みます）ら、ねむく　なります。

3 イギリスへ ＿＿＿＿＿（かえります）も、日本の　ことを　わすれません。

4 ＿＿＿＿＿（けっこんします）ら、いえを　かいます。

5 ＿＿＿＿＿（ちょ金します）も、すぐ　つかって　しまいます。

6 タクシーで ＿＿＿＿＿（行きます）も、間に　あいません。

7 ねつが ＿＿＿＿＿（あります）ら、かいしゃを　休みます。

The conditionals with adjectives and nouns

Adjectives and nouns can also be used in conditional sentences.

い adjectives

大きかったら　*if it was big*

大きくなかったら　*if it wasn't big*

大きくても　*even if it was big*

大きくなくても　*even if it wasn't big*

な adjectives and nouns

しずかだったら　*if it was quiet*

しずかじゃ　なかったら　*if it wasn't quiet*

しずかでも　*even if it was quiet*

しずかじゃ　なくても　*even if it wasn't quiet*

日曜日だったら　*if it was Sunday*

日曜日じゃ　なかったら　*if it wasn't Sunday*

日曜日でも　*even if it was Sunday*

日曜日じゃ　なくても　*even if it wasn't Sunday*

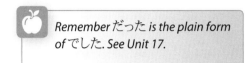
Remember だった *is the plain form of* でした. *See Unit 17.*

D Complete the sentences by choosing the correct words from the box and changing them into the appropriate forms.

> いたいです　あついです　わるいです　りょ行したいです　高いです
> さむいです　つまらないです

1 つごうが ＿＿＿＿ ら、パーティーに　来なくても　いいです。

2 ＿＿＿＿ も、あたらしい　けいたいを　かいます。

3 ＿＿＿＿ ら、しごとを　やめます。

4 ＿＿＿＿ も、まどを　あけないで　ください。

5 あたまが ＿＿＿＿ も、くすりを　飲みません。

6 ＿＿＿＿ ら、まどを　しめて　ください。

7 ＿＿＿＿ ら、ちょ金した　ほうが　いいです。

E Complete the sentences by changing the words in brackets into the appropriate form.

1 ＿＿＿＿（おもしろくないです）も、べんきょうを　つづけます。

2 ＿＿＿＿（いそがしくないです）ら、週まつは　こどもと　あそびます。

3 ＿＿＿＿（ねむいです）も、レポートを　書かなければ　なりません。

4 ＿＿＿＿（いいです）ら、＿＿＿＿（高いです）も、かいます。

5 ＿＿＿＿（おいしくないです）も、食べます。

6 あそびに ＿＿＿＿（行きたいです）も、時間と　お金が　ありません。

F Complete the sentences by choosing the correct words from the box and changing them into the appropriate form.

> 雨^{あめ}です 学生^{がくせい}です ひまです むりです きらいです かんたんです 好^すきです

1 土曜日^{どようび}、＿＿＿＿＿ら、テニスを　しませんか。

2 つかいかたが ＿＿＿＿＿ も、この　ラップトップを　かいません。

3 ＿＿＿＿＿ら、食^たべなくても　いいです。

4 日本^{にほん}りょうりが ＿＿＿＿＿ら、おいしい　レストランが　ありますよ。

5 ＿＿＿＿＿ も、出^でかけます。

6 ＿＿＿＿＿ら、1わりびきです。

7 ＿＿＿＿＿ら、あした　来^こなくても　いいです。

G Complete the sentences by changing the words in brackets into the appropriate form.

1 しごとが＿＿＿＿＿（たいへんです）も、かいしゃを　やめません。

2 ＿＿＿＿＿（下手^{へた}です）も、＿＿＿＿＿（れんしゅうします）ら、上手^{じょうず}に　なります。

3 ＿＿＿＿＿（きらいです）も、食^たべます。

4 ＿＿＿＿＿（きれいです）も、＿＿＿＿＿（やすくないです）ら、かいません。

5 ＿＿＿＿＿（ふべんです）も、車^{くるま}を　つかわないで、電車^{でんしゃ}に　のります。

6 つかれて　いますから、＿＿＿＿＿（いい　天気^{てんき}です）も、どこも　行^いきたくないです。

7 ゆう名^{めい}な＿＿＿＿＿（レストランです）も、＿＿＿＿＿（おいしくないです）ら、
食^たべに　行^いきません。

 # Reading

H Read the following composition written by Mr Tanaka's son, Takashi, describing what he wants to do in future and answer the questions in Japanese. He is in the second grade of high school (age 17).

ぼくは　今、高校二年生です。えい語が　とくいです。しゅみは　ギターを　ひく

ことです。来年　高校を　そつぎょうします。高校を　出ても、すぐ　大学に

入りたくないです。大学に　入る　前に、一年ぐらい　イギリスで　えい語を

べんきょうしたいです。イギリス人の　友だちも　つくりたいです。

大学に　入ったら、べんきょうしながら　アルバイトを　しようと　おもって　います。

ちょ金して、なつ休みに　アジアや　中国を　りょ行したいです。

大学を　出たら、えい語の　きょうしに　なりたいです。そして、やさしくて　あたまが

いい　人と　けっこんしたいです。けっこんしたら、小さい　いえを　かいたいです。

40さいに　なったら、じぶんの　かいしゃを　つくりたいです。60さいに　なったら、

しごとを　やめて、おきなわに　すみたいです。

1 たかしくんは　高校を　出たら、何を　したいと　おもって　いますか。

_____

2 大学に　入ったら、何を　しようと　おもっていますか。

_____

3 どうして　ちょ金しますか。

_____

4 大学を　出たら、何を　したいと　おもって　いますか。

_____

5 どんな　人と　けっこんしたいと　おもって　いますか。

_____

6 けっこんしたら、何を　したいと　おもって　いますか。

_____

7 40さいに　なったら、何を　したいと　おもって　いますか。

_____

ぼく	*I (informal equivalent of* わたし *used by boys)*
そつぎょうします III	*graduate*
じぶん	*self, (my) own*
〜くん	*Mr (informal equivalent of* 〜さん *for boys)*

Writing

I Imagine you are Miss Suzuki and describe your plan. 1) You are currently a bank employee and your hobby is travelling. 2) You enjoy your work, but you are always very busy. Because you don't have free time, you cannot go travelling. 3) You have decided to quit your job as you want to go travelling in Europe for three months. 4) You plan to visit the UK, France and Germany. If you have time, you also want to go to Italy and Spain. 5) Once you return to Japan, you want to start your own company.

Japanese script

We will introduce five kanji in this unit.

KANJI	READING	MEANING	EXAMPLE WORDS
口	くち、ぐち、こう	*mouth*	くち 口 じんこう 人口 *(population)* いりぐち 入口 *(entrance)* でぐち 出口 *(exit)*
東	ひがし、とう	*east*	とう 東きょう ひがしぐち 東口 *(east exit of a station)*
西	にし、せい、さい	*west*	にし 西ヨーロッパ にしぐち 西口 *(west exit)*
南	みなみ、なん	*south*	とうなん 東南アジア みなみぐち 南口 *(south exit)*
北	きた、ほく、ほっ	*north*	ほっかい 北海どう きたぐち 北口 *(north exit)*

J **Choose the correct kanji to complete the sentences.**

六千四百万 行 東南 人口 来週 西口 東 北海 一

1 タイは＿＿＿＿＿＿＿アジアに　あります。

2 ＿＿＿＿＿＿＿の　月曜日に＿＿＿＿＿＿＿きょうへ　かえります。
（げつようび）

3 ＿＿＿＿＿＿＿ど＿＿＿＿＿＿＿どうへ＿＿＿＿＿＿＿って　みたいです。

4 あした　えきの＿＿＿＿＿＿＿で　あいましょう。

5 イギリスの＿＿＿＿＿＿＿は＿＿＿＿＿＿＿人です。
（にん）

Self-check

Tick the box which matches your level of confidence.

1 = very confident   2 = need more practice   3 = not confident

下のボックスにじしんがあるかないかチェックしましょう。

1. じしんがある   2. れんしゅうがひつよう   3. じしんがない

	1	2	3
Expressing *if*, *when*, and *even if* using verbs.			
Expressing *if* and *even if* using adjectives and nouns.			
Recognizing the kanji for *mouth, east, west, south* and *north*.			

*For more information on how to express the conditionals *if* and *when* using verbs, adjectives and nouns refer to *Complete Japanese*, Unit 13.

Unit 1

A

2 たなかさんは　こうむいんです。　Tanaka-san wa kōmuin desu.

3 ロバートさんは　がくせいじゃ　ありません。　Robāto-san wa gakusei ja arimasen.

4 すずきさんは　かんごしじゃ　ありません。　Suzuki-san wa kangoshi ja arimasen.

5 やまださんは　きょうしです。　Yamada-san wa kyōshi desu.

6 アンさんは　いしゃです。　An-san wa isha desu.

7 さとうさんは　ぎんこういんです。　Satō-san wa ginkōin desu.

B

Nationality	Language	Origin of items
にほんじん (Nihon-jin)	にほんご (Nihon-go)	にほんの (Nihon no)
スペインじん (Supein-jin)	スペインご (Supein-go)	スペインの (Supein no)
アメリカじん (Amerika-jin)	えいご (Eigo)	アメリカの (Amerika no)
ちゅうごくじん (Chūgoku-jin)	ちゅうごくご (Chūgoku-go)	ちゅうごくの (Chūgoku no)
ドイツじん (Doitsu-jin)	ドイツご (Doitsu-go)	ドイツの (Doitsu no)
イギリスじん (Igirisu-jin)	えいご (Eigo)	イギリスの (Igirisu no)
イタリアじん (Itaria-jin)	イタリアご (Itaria-go)	イタリアの (Itaria no)
かんこくじん (Kankoku-jin)	かんこくご (Kankoku-go)	かんこくの (Kankoku no)
フランスじん (Furansu-jin)	フランスご (Furansu-go)	フランスの (Furansu no)

C

2 それ (sore) **3** この (kono) **4** あの (ano)、フランスじん (Furansu-jin) **5** それ (sore)、ドイツの (Doitsu no) **6** この (kono)、にほんの (Nihon no)

D

2 ちちは　きょうしです。　Chichi wa kyōshi desu.

3 これは　ははの　とけいです。　Kore wa haha no tokei desu.

4 あの　ひとは　すずきさんの　ごしゅじんです。　Ano hito wa Suzuki-san no go-shujin desu.

5 むすこさんは　がくせいですか。　Musuko-san wa gakusei desu ka.

6 たなかさんの　おくさんは　イギリスじんです。　Tanaka-san no okusan wa Igirisu-jin desu.

E

1 English/British **2** Company employee **3** Bank worker **4** Two (sons)

F

1 わたし 2 にほんじん 3 ワイン 4 ごしゅじん 5 じゅうに

H

1 日本人 2 人(にん) 3 日本 4 私, 人(にん) 5 人(ひと) 6 月, 日, 日よう日

Unit 2

A

2 テレビ (terebi), を 3 あさごはん (asa gohan), を 4 かいしゃ (kaisha), へ 5 しんぶん (shinbun), を 6 日本ご(にほん) (Nihon-go), を 7 ビール (bīru), を 8 うち (uchi), へ 9 テニス (tenisu), を

B

2 へ 3 で 4 へ 5 へ 6 で 7 で 8 で

C

1 に 2 ×, に 3 に 4 ×, に 5 ×, ×, × 6 ×

D

1 は, に, と, を 2 で, を 3 ×, を 4 ×, へ 5 ×, に 6 で, から, まで

E

2

A: いっしょに　テニスを　しませんか。　Issho ni tenisu o shimasen ka.

B: はい、しましょう。Hai, shimashō.

3

A: いっしょに　えいがを　みませんか。　Issho ni eiga o mimasen ka.

B: はい、みましょう。　Hai, mimashō.

4

A: いっしょに　ビールを　のみませんか。　Issho ni bīru o nomimasen ka.

B: はい、のみましょう。　Hai, nomimashō.

5

A: いっしょに　きょうとへ　いきませんか。　Issho ni Kyōto e ikimasen ka.

B: はい、いきましょう。Hai, ikimashō.

F

1 たなかさんは、まいあさ　7じに　おきます。　Tanaka-san wa maiasa shichi-ji ni okimasu.

2 いいえ、あさごはんは　たべません。　Iie, asa gohan wa tabemasen.

3 いつも　かいしゃで　ひるごはんを　たべます。　Itsumo kaisha de hiru gohan o tabemasu.

4 テレビを　みます。　Terebi o mimasu.

5 ときどき　ブログを　かきます。　Tokidoki burogu o kakimasu.

G

3 私は　よく　ともだちと　ビールを　のみます。　Watashi wa yoku tomodachi to bīru o nomimasu.

4 たなかさんは　あまり　テレビを　みません。　Tanaka-san wa amari terebi o mimasen.

5 私は　ぜんぜん　ラジオを　ききません。　Watashi wa zenzen rajio o kikimasen.

6 私は　たいてい　うちで　えいがを　みます。　Watashi wa taitei uchi de eiga o mimasu.

7 ロバートさんは　ときどき　8じまで　はたらきます。　Robāto-san wa tokidoki hachi-ji made hatarakimasu.

H

1 きょう　2 かえります　3 ぎんこう　4 日本ご　5 テニス

J

1 I work from Monday to Friday.

2 I go to Japanese language school on Tuesday and Thursday.

3 I play tennis on Wednesday.

4 I have dinner with my friend on Saturday.

5 I often go to an art gallery on Sunday.

Unit 3

A

1 こうえんに　おとこの　人が　います。　Kōen ni otoko no hito ga imasu.

2 いまに　テレビが　あります。　Ima ni terebi ga arimasu.

3 にわに　いぬと　ねこが　います。｜にわに　ねこと　いぬが　います。　Niwa ni inu to neko ga imasu./Niwa ni neko to inu ga imasu.

4 あそこに　おんなの　人が　います。　Asoko ni onna no hito ga imasu.

5 この　へやに　コンピューターが　あります。　Kono heya ni konpyūtā ga arimasu.

6 レストランに　おとこの　こと　おんなの　こが　います。｜レストランに　おんなの　こと　おとこの　こが　います。　Resutoran ni otoko no ko to onna no ko ga imasu. / Resutoran ni onna no ko to otoko no ko ga imasu.

B

2 この　かばんの　なかに　けいたいや　とけい　などが　あります。　Kono kaban no naka ni kētai ya tokei nado ga arimasu.

3 デパートの　よこに　本やが　あります。　Depāto no yoko ni honya ga arimasu.

4 この　はこの　なかに　くつが　あります。　Kono hako no naka ni kutsu ga arimasu.

5 えきの　まえに　じどうはんばいきが　あります。　Eki no mae ni jidōhanbaiki ga arimasu.

6 その　つくえの　うえに　本が　あります。　Sono tsukue no ue ni hon ga arimasu.

7 あの　木の　したに　おとこの　こと　おんなの　こが　います。　Ano ki no shita ni otoko no ko to onna no ko ga imasu.

8 えきの　ちかくに　ぎんこうが　あります。　Eki no chikaku ni ginkō ga arimasu.

C

2 はっぽん (happon)　**3** さんびき (san-biki)　**4** にだい (ni-dai)　**5** ななつ (nanatsu)　**6** ろくまい (roku-mai)　**7** ごにん (go-nin)

D

1 や, や, が　**2** に, の, に　**3** に, が, も　**4** ×, の, に, が, が, ×

E

チケット (chiketto), しごと (shigoto), やくそく (yakusoku), じかん (jikan)

F

2 さんぜんろっぴゃく (sanzen roppyaku)　**3** ろっぴゃくよんじゅうに (roppyaku yonjū ni)
4 ななまんきゅうせんにひゃく (nanaman kyūsen nihyaku)　**5** いちまんはっせんはっぴゃく (ichiman hassen happyaku)　**6** ごひゃくじゅう (gohyaku jū)　**7** ごまんにせんひゃくろくじゅうなな (goman nisen hyaku rokujū nana)

G

1 ロバートさんは　デパートへ　いきます。(Robāto-san wa depāto e ikimasu)

2 デパートは　えきの　まえに　あります。(depāto wa eki no mae ni arimasu)

3 イタリアの　ネクタイは　8,000えんです。(Itaria no nekutai wa 8,000-en desu)

4 フランスの　ネクタイは　5,000えんです。(Furansu no nekutai wa 5,000-en desu)

H

1 にわ 2 そこ 3 れいぞうこ 4 いま 5 本<ruby>本<rt>ほん</rt></ruby>や 6 レストラン

J

1 男(女), 子, 女(男), 子 2 円 3 中, 本

Unit 4

A

Present	Present negative	Past	Past negative
おきます okimasu	おきません okimasen	おきました okimashita	おきませんでした okimasen deshita
ねます nemasu	ねません nemasen	ねました nemashita	ねませんでした nemasen deshita
はたらきます hatarakimasu	はたらきません hatarakimasen	はたらきました hatarakimashita	はたらきませんでした hatarakimasen deshita
いきます ikimasu	いきません ikimasen	いきました ikimashita	いきませんでした ikimasen deshita
きます kimasu	きません kimasen	きました kimashita	きませんでした kimasen deshita
かえります kaerimasu	かえりません kaerimasen	かえりました kaerimashita	かえりませんでした kaerimasen deshita
します shimasu	しません shimasen	しました shimashita	しませんでした shimasen deshita
たべます tabemasu	たべません tabemasen	たべました tabemashita	たべませんでした tabemasen deshita
のみます nomimasu	のみません nomimasen	のみました nomimashita	のみませんでした nomimasen deshita
みます mimasu	みません mimasen	みました mimashita	みませんでした mimasen deshita
ききます kikimasu	ききません kikimasen	ききました kikimashita	ききませんでした kikimasen deshita
よみます yomimasu	よみません yomimasen	よみました yomimashita	よみませんでした yomimasen deshita

かきます	かきません	かきました	かきませんでした
kakimasu	kakimasen	kakimashita	kakimasen deshita
べんきょうします	べんきょうしません	べんきょうしました	べんきょうしませんでした
benkyō shimasu	benkyō shimasen	benkyō shimashita	benkyō shimasen deshita

B

1 あいました 2 いきます 3 はなしました 4 のみません 5 たべませんでした 6 かいました

C

1 ×, に, へ 2 に, に, を 3 に, から, まで 4 の, で, を 5 と, に, を 6 に, に, を

D

1 くれました 2 もらいました 3 あげました 4 あげました 5 くれました 6 もらいました

E

3 じゅうにじよんじゅうごふん (jūni-ji yonjū go-fun) 4 しちじじゅうはっぷん (shichi-ji jū happun)
5 くじにじゅうきゅうふん (ku-ji nijū kyū-fun) 6 よじにふん (yo-ji ni-fun) 7 はちじじゅうごふん (hachi-ji jūgo-fun) 8 にじごじゅっぷん (ni-ji go juppun)

F

2 しがつ　にじゅうごにち 3 いちがつ　ついたち 4 じゅうにがつ　にじゅうよっか
5 ろくがつ　じゅうろくにち 6 ごがつ　いつか 7 くがつ　とおか 8 じゅういちがつ
じゅうはちにち 9 しちがつ　なのか

G

3 コーヒーを　のみたいです。　Kōhī o nomitai desu.

4 うちへ　かえりたいです。　Uchi e kaeritai desu.

5 ひるごはんを　たべたいです。　Hiru gohan o tabetai desu.

6 えいがを　みたいです。　Eiga o mitai desu.

7 ともだちに　あいたいです。　Tomodachi ni aitai desu.

8 プレゼントを　あげたいです。　Purezento o agetai desu.

9 ケーキを　かいたいです。　Kēki o kaitai desu.

H

1 しぶやへ　いきました。Shibuya e ikimashita.

2 えいがを　みました。それから　ばんごはんを　たべました。Eiga o mimashita. Sorekara ban gohan o tabemashita.

3 ロバートさんの　うちで　パーティーが　あります。Robāto-san no uchi de pātī ga arimasu.

4 デパートで　ネクタイを　かいます。それから　パーティーへ　いきます。Depāto de nekutai o kaimasu. Sorekara pātī e ikimasu.

I

1 たんじょうび　**2** なんじ　**3** かいます　**4** せんしゅう　**5** ごはん　**6** くつ

K

1 何時　**2** 時, 分　**3** 何, 食　**4** 飲　**5** 日, 何月何日

Unit 5

A

Affirmative form	Negative form	Connecting two adjectives	Before nouns
いい	よくない	よくて	いい
わるい	わるくない	わるくて	わるい
おおきい	おおきくない	おおきくて	おおきい
ちいさい	ちいさくない	ちいさくて	ちいさい
たかい	たかくない	たかくて	たかい
ひくい	ひくくない	ひくくて	ひくい
やすい	やすくない	やすくて	やすい
ながい	ながくない	ながくて	ながい
みじかい	みじかくない	みじかくて	みじかい
おいしい	おいしくない	おいしくて	おいしい
おもしろい	おもしろくない	おもしろくて	おもしろい
むずかしい	むずかしくない	むずかしくて	むずかしい
いそがしい	いそがしくない	いそがしくて	いそがしい
たのしい	たのしくない	たのしくて	たのしい

B

Affirmative form	Negative form	Connecting two adjectives	Before nouns
ゆうめい	ゆうめいじゃ　ない	ゆうめいで	ゆうめいな
にぎやか	にぎやかじゃ　ない	にぎやかで	にぎやかな
きれい	きれいじゃ　ない	きれいで	きれいな
しずか	しずかじゃ　ない	しずかで	しずかな
しんせつ	しんせつじゃ　ない	しんせつで	しんせつな
げんき	げんきじゃ　ない	げんきで	げんきな
ひま	ひまじゃ　ない	ひまで	ひまな
べんり	べんりじゃ　ない	べんりで	べんりな
すてき	すてきじゃ　ない	すてきで	すてきな

C

1 な　2 ×,×　3 ×　4 ×　5 な　6 な　7 ×

D

2 おいしくて　やすいです。 3 しんせつで　すてきです。 4 いそがしくて　たのしくないです。
5 しずかで　きれいです。 6 にぎやかで　たのしいです。 7 ながくて　むずかしいです。

E

3 おいしいですが、たかいです。 4 いそがしいですが、たのしいです。 5 おもしろくて　たのしいです。
6 おもしろいですが　むずかしいです。 7 やすくて　いいです。/やすいですが、いいです。

F

2 あたまが　よくて　しんせつな　人(ひと)です。 3 めが　おおきくて　きれいな　人(ひと)です。 4 せが
ひくくて　おもしろい　人(ひと)です。 5 かみが　みじかくて　すてきな　人(ひと)です。 6 にぎやかで　たのしい
ところです。

G

1 何(なに)　2 だれ　3 どう　4 どこ　5 いくら　6 何(なん)　7 どんな

H

1 とても　いそがしいですが、あまり　むずかしくないです。

2 せが　たかくて、しんせつな　人(ひと)です。

3 かみが　ながくて　すてきな　人<ruby>人<rt>ひと</rt></ruby>です。

4 やすくて　おいしい　レストランが　あります。

5 レストランへ　いきます。

I

1 × **2** だ　**3** × **4** × **5** だ　**6** だ

J

1 きれい　**2** ゆうめい　**3** いい　**4** べんり　**5** ひと　**6** せ

L

1 大　**2** 小　**3** 高　**4** 低　**5** 長

Unit 6

A

Present affirmative	Past affirmative	Past negative
いいです	よかったです	よくなかったです
おいしいです	おいしかったです	おいしくなかったです
たのしいです	たのしかったです	たのしくなかったです
すばらしいです	すばらしかったです	すばらしくなかったです
つまらないです	つまらなかったです	つまらなくなかったです
おおいです	おおかったです	おおくなかったです
すくないです	すくなかったです	すくなくなかったです
あたたかいです	あたたかかったです	あたたかくなかったです
あついです	あつかったです	あつくなかったです
すずしいです	すずしかったです	すずしくなかったです
さむいです	さむかったです	さむくなかったです

B

2 きのうは　あたたかかったです。**3** とうきょうは　ひとが　おおかったです。
4 えいがは　つまらなかったです。**5** びじゅつかんは　すばらしかったです。
6 せんしゅうは　さむくなかったです。**7** きのうは　あつかったです。

C

Present affirmative	Past affirmative	Past negative
しずかです	しずかでした	しずかじゃ　なかったです
きれいです	きれいでした	きれいじゃ　なかったです
にぎやかです	にぎやかでした	にぎやかじゃ　なかったです
たいへんです	たいへんでした	たいへんじゃ　なかったです
かんたんです	かんたんでした	かんたんじゃ　なかったです
いやです	いやでした	いやじゃ　なかったです

D

Present affirmative	Past affirmative	Past negative
いい　てんきです	いい　てんきでした	いい　てんきじゃ　なかったです
いやな　てんきです	いやな　てんきでした	いやな　てんきじゃ　なかったです
あめです	あめでした	あめじゃ　なかったです
ゆきです	ゆきでした	ゆきじゃ　なかったです
くもりです	くもりでした	くもりじゃ　なかったです

E

2 きのうは　あめでした。 3 せん月（げつ）の　テストは　かんたんでした。 4 しごとは　たいへんでした。
5 せんしゅうは　いやな　てんきでした。 6 おとといは　くもりでした。

F

2 ながくて　つまらなかったです。 3 いい　てんきでしたが、人（ひと）が　おおかったです。
4 おもしろくて　すばらしかったです。 5 みじかかったですが、たのしかったです。
6 やすかったですが、おいしくなかったです。 7 にぎやかで　きれいでした。

G

1 で,へ　2 から,で　3 の,×　4 から,で,へ　5 ×,で,へ　6 から,まで,で　7 と,で,へ　8 で,へ

H

1 きよみずでらへ　いきました。

2 しんかんせんと　タクシーで　いきました。

3 レストランや　みせが　たくさん　あります。

4 とても　にぎやかで、きれいでしたが、とても　あつかったです。

I

あたたかく, あつく, すずしく, さむい

J

1 きのう 2 おいしい 3 いや 4 たいへん 5 えき 6 せんしゅう

L

1 天気 2 土, 日, 雨 3 車, 高 4 私, 気 5 電車

Unit 7

A

1 わたしは　あたらしい　コンピューターが　ほしいです。2 ちちは　りょうりが　へたです。

3 ロバートさんは　カラオケが　じょうずです。4 すずきさんは　えいごが　分かりません。

5 たなかさんは　車が　あります。6 つまは　ビールが　きらいです。

7 すずきさんは　日本りょうりが　すきです。8 たなかさんは　すうがくが　とくいです。

9 すずきさんは　えいごが　にがてです。

B

2

たなか:	どんな　おんがくが　すきですか。
ロバート:	私は　ロックが　すきです。
すずき:	私は　クラシックが　すきです。たなかさんは。
たなか:	私は　ジャズが　すきです。

3

たなか:	どんな　飲みものが　すきですか。
ロバート:	私は　ビールが　すきです。
すずき:	私は　ワインが　すきです。たなかさんは。
たなか:	私は　コーヒーが　すきです。

4

たなか:	どんな　食べものが　すきですか。
ロバート:	私は　にくが　すきです。
すずき:	私は　やさいが　すきです。たなかさんは。
たなか:	私は　さかなが　すきです。

C

1 すき, はる, すき 2 りょうり, じょうず, はは, りょうり, じょうず 3 おもしろかった, きょうと, おもしろかった
4 ほしい, お金（かね）, ほしい

D

2 エドワードさんは　日本（にほん）ごが　よく　分（わ）かります。
3 すずきさんは　ちゅうごくごが　ぜんぜん　分（わ）かりません。
4 アンさんは　かたかなが　だいたい　分（わ）かります。
5 ロバートさんは　かんじが　あまり　分（わ）かりません。

E

1 飲（の）みたかった 2 食（た）べ 3 したくない 4 かきかた 5 ききながら 6 あそび 7 かえりたい 8 みながら

F

1 はい、ひまです。

2 カラオケを　しに　いきます。| カラオケを　します。

3 はい、すきです。

4 いいえ、あまり　しません。

H

1 好 2 語 3 下手(上手) 4 日本語, 上手(下手) 5 下 6 上

Unit 8

A

Group I: まがります、つくります、はいります、つかいます、まちます、もちます、しにます、えらびます、やすみます、およぎます、いそぎます、けします

Group II: とめます、でます、でかけます、おしえます、みせます、つけます

B

ます form	て form	English
あいます	あって	*meet*
もらいます	もらって	*receive*
つかいます	つかって	*use*
かいます	かって	*buy*
おもいます	おもって	*think*

まちます	まって	*wait*
もちます	もって	*hold, carry*

かえります	かえって	*return*
分かります	分かって	*understand*
はいります	はいって	*enter*
あります	あって	*be, exist*
つくります	つくって	*make*
まがります	まがって	*turn*

C

ます form	て form	English
飲みます	飲んで	*drink*
やすみます	やすんで	*rest*
よみます	よんで	*read*

あそびます	あそんで	*play*
えらびます	えらんで	*choose*

しにます	しんで	*die*

D

ます form	て form	English
はたらきます	はたらいて	*work*
かきます	かいて	*write*
ききます	きいて	*listen*

いきます	いって	*go*

およぎます	およいで	*swim*
いそぎます	いそいで	*hurry*

E

ます form	て form	English
はなします	はなして	*talk*
けします	けして	*turn off*

F

ます form	て form	English
ねます	ねて	*sleep*
あげます	あげて	*give*
みせます	みせて	*show*
おしえます	おしえて	*tell, teach*
とめます	とめて	*stop, park (a vehicle)*
食べます	食べて	*eat*
くれます	くれて	*give me*
でかけます	でかけて	*go out*
でます	でて	*exit*
つけます	つけて	*turn on*

おきます	おきて	*wake up*
います	いて	*be, exist*
みます	みて	*see, watch*

G

ます form	て form	English
します	して	*do*
べんきょうします	べんきょうして	*study*
きます	きて	*come*

H

1 あって, みて 2 いって, およいで 3 つくって, はいって 4 でて, はたらいて 5 よんで, かいて, はなして

I

2 その とけいを みせて ください。 3 この かんじの よみかたを おしえて ください。
4 この コンピューターを つかって ください。 5 まって ください。

6 この　かばんを　もって　ください。7 飲みものを　えらんで　ください。8いそいで　ください。9 テレビを　けして　ください。

J

1 ロバートさんの　うちへ　いきます。

2 すずきさんの　車で　いきます。

3 こうえんの　まえです。

4 あたらしくて　すてきな　うちです。

5 ピザを　食べて、えいがを　みます。

K

1 飲みます　2いきます　3きます　4あそびます　5しんごう

M

1 来,行　2 来　3 行,右(左)　4 左(右)　5 見

Unit 9

A

Group I

ます form	て form
おきます	おいて
たちます	たって
すわります	すわって
とります	とって
すいます	すって
かします	かして

Group II

ます form	て form
あけます	あけて
しめます	しめて
かります	かりて

Group III

ます form	て form
うんてんします	うんてんして

B

1 あけて 2 すわって 3 かえって 4 しめて 5 おいて 6 かりて

C

1 すって 2 とめて 3 はいって 4 とって 5 のんで, うんてんして

D

1 に 2 で 3 に 4 に 5 で 6 に 7 で

E

1 べんきょうし, 行き 2 たって 3 かして 4 飲んで, およいで 5 よみ, おしえて 6 つかい, うんてんして 7 飲み, 見 8 かえって

F

3, 1, 4, 2

G

1 20さいから　おさけを　飲んでも　いいです。

2 きつえんせきで　すっても　いいです。

3 18さいから　うんてんしても　いいです。

4 16さいから　けっこんしても　いいです。

H

2 ひだり 3 さむい 4 小さい 5 低い | やすい 6 けします 7 ねます 8 かります 9 しめます
10 すわります

I

1 およぎます (other verbs trigger the particle に after place names) 2 コーヒー 3 かします 4 まど
5 話します 6 かります

K

1 来, 行 2 右 3 土, 日, 休 4 話, 5 出, 6 入

Unit 10

A

Group I

ます form	て form
ふります	ふって
ならいます	ならって
うります	うって
しります	しって
すみます	すんで

Group II

ます form	て form
かけます	かけて
きます	きて

Group III

ます form	て form
れんらくします	れんらくして

B

2 いま 雨（あめ）が ふって います。**3** ロバートさんは いま 電話（でんわ）を かけて います。**4** 私（わたし）は いま おんがくを きいて います。**5** 私（わたし）は いま 休（やす）んで います。**6** ロバートさんは たなかさんと 話（はな）して いました。**7** すずきさんは しんぶんを よんで いました。

C

1 して います **2** ならって います **3** かりて います **4** かいて います **5** つくって います

D

1 どこで やすい コンピューターを うって いますか。

2 まい日（にち） 9時（じ）から 5時（じ）まで はたらいて います。

3 えい語（ご）の がっこうで えい語（ご）を べんきょうして います。

4 すずきさんは ぎん行（こう）で はたらいて います。

5 まいあさ　やさいで　しんせんな　ジュースを　つくって　います。

6 私（わたし）は　大（だい）がくで　日本語（にほんご）を　おしえて　います。

7 あの　みせで　何（なに）を　うって　いますか。

8 いつも　メイルで　くにの　かぞくに　れんらくして　います。

E

1 いいえ、しりません。

2 いいえ、けっこんして　いません。

3 しんじゅくに　すんで　います。

4 たいてい　うちで　えいがを　見（み）て　います。

5 たなかさんと　ロバートさんと　よこはまへ　車（くるま）で　あそびに　行（い）きます。

F

3 B　**4** B　**5** B　**6** A　**7** A

G

1 b, c　**2** b, c, a　**3** c, b

H

2 (1)　**3** (4)　**4** (5)　**5** (2)　**6** (5)　**7** (3)

K

1 今, 入　**2** 学校, 話　**3** 見, 食　**4** 今日, 出, 休　**5** 学生　**6** 今

Unit 11

A

1 月（つき）へ　行（い）って　みたいです。　**2** この　くつを　はいて　みても　いいですか。

3 もう　いちど　かんがえて　みます。　**4** あの　しろい　コートを　きて　みても　いいですか。

5 きのう　はじめて　すしを　食（た）べて　みました。　**6** その　ぼうしを　かぶって　みたいです。

B

2 パスポートを　わすれて　しまいました。**3** さいふを　おとして　しまいました。

4 この　しごとを　やって　しまいます。**5** みちを　まちがえて　しまいました。

6 こんばん　この　レポートを　かいて　しまいます。

7 ケーキを　ぜんぶ　食（た）べて　しまいました。

C

2 私は　ロバートさんに　本を　かして　あげました。

3 私は　ロバートさんに　ケーキを　つくって　あげました。

4 私は　ロバートさんに　かんじの　いみを　せつめいして　あげました。

5 私は　ロバートさんに　ジェームスさんを　しょうかいして　あげました。

6 私は　ロバートさんに　りょこうの　しゃしんを　見せて　あげました。

D

1 c　2 b　3 a　4 b　5 a　6 a

E

2 たなかさんは　私に　ジェームスさんを　しょうかいして　くれました。

3 すずきさんは　私に　りょこうの　しゃしんを　見せて　くれました。

4 ロバートさんは　私に　お金を　かして　くれました。

5 ちちは　私に　あたらしい　スーツを　かって　くれました。

6 すずきさんは　私に　おいしい　日本りょうりを　つくって　くれました。

F

1 たなかさんは　あさくさに　すんでいます。

2 いいえ、分かりませんでした。| いいえ、みちを　まちがえて　しまいました。

3 いいえ、しりませんでした。

4 よこはまへ　行きました。

5 いいえ、雨が　ふって　いました。

6 たなかさんの　おくさんに　つくって　もらいました。

7 かまくらへ　行きたいです。

G

2 e, きます　3 g, きます　4 f, はきます　5 b, きます　6 d, はきます　7 c, はきます

H

2 (4)　3 (2)　4 (3)　5 (1)　6 (5)

J

1 日本語　2 学校, 先生, 話　3 車, 行　4 学生　5 父(母), 母(父)　6 先, 白

Unit 12

A

ます form	Plain form	English
かいます	かう	*buy*
あいます	あう	*meet*
まちます	まつ	*wait*
もちます	もつ	*hold, carry*
かえります	かえる	*return*
はいります	はいる	*enter*
飲みます	飲む	*drink*
よみます	よむ	*read*
あそびます	あそぶ	*play*
えらびます	えらぶ	*choose*
はたらきます	はたらく	*work*
行きます	行く	*go*
およぎます	およぐ	*swim*
いそぎます	いそぐ	*hurry*
話します	話す	*talk*
けします	けす	*turn off*

B

ます form	Plain form	English
ねます	ねる	*sleep*
かけます	かける	*make (a phone call)*
食べます	食べる	*eat*
出かけます	出かける	*go out*
見ます	見る	*see, watch*
かります	かりる	*borrow*
おきます	おきる	*wake up*
きます	きる	*wear, put on*

C

ます form	Plain form	English
します	する	*do*
りょこうします	りょこうする	*travel*
うんてんします	うんてんする	*drive*
来〈き〉ます	来〈く〉る	*come*

D

2 学校〈がっこう〉へ 行〈い〉く まえに、コーヒーを 飲〈の〉みます。

3 ひるごはんを 食〈た〉べる まえに、しんぶんを よみます。 4 出〈で〉かける まえに、電話〈でんわ〉を かけます。

5 おふろに 入〈はい〉る まえに、ブログを かきます。 6 レポートを かく まえに、メイルを よみます。

7 ビールを 飲〈の〉む まえに、おふろに 入〈はい〉ります。

E

のぼる, とる, よむ, 見〈み〉る, ひく, りょこうする, かく

F

1 話〈はな〉す こと 2 およぐ こと 3 つかう こと 4 つくる こと 5 のぼる こと 6 ひく こと
7 よむ こと 8 はらう こと 9 かく こと

G

1 3ねんまえに 日本〈にほん〉へ 来〈き〉ました。

2 いそがしいですが、とても たのしいです。

3 はい、かく ことが できます。

4 うんてんする ことと およぐ ことです。

5 車〈くるま〉が ありませんから。

6 ジムへ 行〈い〉って、およいで います。

H

1 ふじさん 2 月〈つき〉 3 来〈く〉る 4 食〈た〉べる 5 する 6 カード

J

1 書 2 先生, 読 3 父, 聞 4 白 5 入, 前, 食

Unit 13

A

きのう	きょう 今日	あした
(yesterday)	(today)	(tomorrow)
せん 先しゅう	こん 今しゅう	らい 来しゅう
(last week)	(this week)	(next week)
せんげつ 先月	こんげつ 今月	らいげつ 来月
(last month)	(this month)	(next month)
きょねん	ことし	らい 来ねん
(last year)	(this year)	(next year)

B

1 行く 2 べんきょうする 3 すんで　みる 4 かって　あげる 5 出かける 6 話す

C

1 りょ行する 2 のぼる 3 けっこんする 4 おわる 5 はじまる 6 はたらく

D

1 b 2 c 3 c 4 b 5 a 6 c

E

1 ベジタリアンな 2 りょ行する 3 ある 4 てつだう 5 すみたい 6 見る

F

1 大さかに　すんで　います。

2 いそがしいです。

3 なつです。

4 ともだちと　いっしょに　りょ行します。

5 とうきょうで　びじゅつかんへ　行く　よていです。

6 来しゅうの　日よう日に　あいたいです。

H

1 外国 2 友,見 3 国 4 名前,書 5 名

Unit 14

A

ます form	て form	Plain past tense	English
かいます	かって	かった	*buy*
つかいます	つかって	つかった	*use*
まちます	まって	まった	*wait*
もちます	もって	もった	*hold, carry*
かえります	かえって	かえった	*return*
のぼります	のぼって	のぼった	*climb*
飲みます	飲んで	飲んだ	*drink*
休みます	休んで	休んだ	*rest*
あそびます	あそんで	あそんだ	*play*
えらびます	えらんで	えらんだ	*choose*
しにます	しんで	しんだ	*die*
はたらきます	はたらいて	はたらいた	*work*
聞きます	聞いて	聞いた	*listen*
行きます	行って	行った	*go*
およぎます	およいで	およいだ	*swim*
いそぎます	いそいで	いそいだ	*hurry*
話します	話して	話した	*talk*
かします	かして	かした	*lend*

B

1 行った 2 のぼった 3 すんだ 4 飲んだ 5 まった 6 あった

C

ます form	て form	Plain past tense	English
ねます	ねて	ねた	*sleep*
食べます	食べて	食べた	*eat*
見せます	見せて	見せた	*show*
おしえます	おしえて	おしえた	*teach*
わすれます	わすれて	わすれた	*forget*

<ruby>出<rt>で</rt></ruby>かけます	<ruby>出<rt>で</rt></ruby>かけて	<ruby>出<rt>で</rt></ruby>かけた	*go out*
かんがえます	かんがえて	かんがえた	*think, consider*
おきます	おきて	おきた	*wake up*
<ruby>見<rt>み</rt></ruby>ます	<ruby>見<rt>み</rt></ruby>て	<ruby>見<rt>み</rt></ruby>た	*see*
います	いて	いた	*be*
かります	かりて	かりた	*borrow*

D

ます form	て form	Plain past tense	English
します	して	した	*do*
りょ<ruby>行<rt>こう</rt></ruby>します	りょ<ruby>行<rt>こう</rt></ruby>して	りょ<ruby>行<rt>こう</rt></ruby>した	*travel*
べんきょうします	べんきょうして	べんきょうした	*study*
せつめいします	せつめいして	せつめいした	*explain*
<ruby>来<rt>き</rt></ruby>ます	<ruby>来<rt>き</rt></ruby>て	<ruby>来<rt>き</rt></ruby>た	*come*

E

1 りょ<ruby>行<rt>こう</rt></ruby>した　2 <ruby>見<rt>み</rt></ruby>た　3 <ruby>食<rt>た</rt></ruby>べた　4 わすれた　5 した　6 <ruby>来<rt>き</rt></ruby>た

F

1 <ruby>行<rt>い</rt></ruby>った　2 <ruby>行<rt>い</rt></ruby>った　3 <ruby>行<rt>い</rt></ruby>きました　4 <ruby>行<rt>い</rt></ruby>った　5 <ruby>書<rt>か</rt></ruby>きました　6 <ruby>食<rt>か</rt></ruby>べました　7 <ruby>食<rt>か</rt></ruby>べて　いません

G

2 ばんごはんを　<ruby>食<rt>た</rt></ruby>べた　あとで、テレビを　<ruby>見<rt>み</rt></ruby>ました。

3 メイルを　<ruby>読<rt>よ</rt></ruby>んだ　あとで、レポートを　<ruby>書<rt>か</rt></ruby>きます。

4 べんきょうした　あとで、CDを　<ruby>聞<rt>き</rt></ruby>きました。

5 おふろに　<ruby>入<rt>はい</rt></ruby>った　あとで、ビールを　<ruby>飲<rt>の</rt></ruby>みます。

6 しごとが　おわった　あとで、カラオケに　<ruby>行<rt>い</rt></ruby>きます。

H

2 エドワードさんは　<ruby>何<rt>なん</rt></ruby>かいか　<ruby>大<rt>おお</rt></ruby>さかへ　<ruby>行<rt>い</rt></ruby>った　ことが　あります。

3 エドワードさんは　いちども　スキーを　した　ことが　ありません。

4 エドワードさんは　<ruby>前<rt>まえ</rt></ruby>に　<ruby>中学校<rt>ちゅうがっこう</rt></ruby>で　はたらいた　ことが　あります。

5 エドワードさんは　ぜんぜん　<ruby>日本<rt>にほん</rt></ruby>の　おさけを　<ruby>飲<rt>の</rt></ruby>んだ　ことが　ありません。

6 エドワードさんは　いちど　ふじさんに　のぼった　ことが　あります。

I

1 今、コンピューターの　かいしゃで　はたらいて　います。

2 今までに　アメリカ、ヨーロッパ、そして　アジアに　行った　ことが　あります。

3 えい語の　きょうしとして　はたらいた　ことが　あります。

4 ふじさんに　のぼった　ことが　あります。すもうを　見に　行った　ことも　あります。おんせんに　入った　ことも　あります。

K

1 前　**2** 時間,友　**3** 後,飲　**4** 外国,行　**5** 山　**6** 来年

Unit 15

A

1 飲んだ,食べた　**2** のぼった,およいだ　**3** した,見た　**4** あそんだ,出かけた　**5** 読んだ,書いた
6 行った,見た

B

2 くすりを　飲んだ　ほうが　いいですよ。　**3** たばこを　やめた　ほうが　いいですよ。　**4** まいあさ
あさごはんを　食べた　ほうが　いいですよ。　**5** すこし　休んだ　ほうが　いいですよ。
6 はやく　ねた　ほうが　いいですよ。

C

2 たなかさんより　ロバートさんの　ほうが　せが　高いです。　　*Robert is taller than Mr Tanaka.*

3 ロバートさんより　すずきさんの　ほうが　わかいです。　　*Miss Suzuki is younger than Robert.*

4 えいがより　本の　ほうが　おもしろいです。　　*Books are more interesting than movies.*

5 ご前より　ご後の　ほうが　ひまです。　　*I have more time in the afternoon than in the morning.*

6 ロンドンより　とうきょうの　ほうが　人が　おおいです。　　*There are more people in Tokyo than in London.*

7 すずきさんより　やまだ先生の　ほうが　げん気です。　　*Mr Yamada is more cheerful than Miss Suzuki.*

8 手がみを　書くより　メイルを　書く　ほうが　べんりです。　　*Writing e-mails is more convenient than writing letters.*

D

1 c 2 a 3 b 4 c 5 a

E

1 りょ<ruby>行<rt>こう</rt></ruby>する 2 りょ<ruby>行<rt>こう</rt></ruby>した 3 <ruby>飲<rt>の</rt></ruby>んだ 4 <ruby>出<rt>で</rt></ruby>る 5 かえる 6 のぼった

F

1 こうちに　すんで　いました。

2 よく　<ruby>山<rt>やま</rt></ruby>に　のぼったり、うみで　およいだり　しました。

3 いつも　<ruby>友<rt>とも</rt></ruby>だちと　<ruby>飲<rt>の</rt></ruby>みに　<ruby>行<rt>い</rt></ruby>ったり、アルバイトを　したり　して　いましたから。

4 ITの　かいしゃに　<ruby>入<rt>はい</rt></ruby>って　3<ruby>年後<rt>ねんご</rt></ruby>に、かずこさんと　けっこんしました。

5 よく　<ruby>子<rt>こ</rt></ruby>どもと　あそんだり、おくさんと　<ruby>出<rt>で</rt></ruby>かけたり　して　います。

G

1 <ruby>学生<rt>がくせい</rt></ruby> 2 みせ 3 べんきょう 4 けいたい 5 わかい

I

1 午,午 2 毎 3 川,川 4 海 5 休,山 6 毎年,行 7 前,本,読

Unit 16

A

ます form	Plain form	English
かいます	かおう	*buy*
あいます	あおう	*meet*
まちます	まとう	*wait*
もちます	もとう	*hold, carry*
かえります	かえろう	*return*
<ruby>入<rt>はい</rt></ruby>ります	<ruby>入<rt>はい</rt></ruby>ろう	*enter*
<ruby>飲<rt>の</rt></ruby>みます	<ruby>飲<rt>の</rt></ruby>もう	*drink*
<ruby>読<rt>よ</rt></ruby>みます	<ruby>読<rt>よ</rt></ruby>もう	*read*
あそびます	あそぼう	*play*
えらびます	えらぼう	*choose*
はたらきます	はたらこう	*work*

行きます	行こう	*go*
およぎます	およごう	*swim*
いそぎます	いそごう	*hurry*
話します	話そう	*talk*
けします	けそう	*turn off*

B

2 休もう *I am tired. Let's have a break.* 3 行こう *Let's go to school early tomorrow.*

4 あおう *Let's meet at the station at 6 p.m. tonight.* 5 書いて　しまおう *Let's finish writing this report.*

6 あそびに　行こう *Let's go to Osaka to have fun.*

C

ます form	Plain form	English
ねます	ねよう	*sleep*
かけます	かけよう	*make (a phone call)*
食べます	食べよう	*eat*
でかけます	でかけよう	*go out*
見ます	見よう	*see, watch*
かります	かりよう	*borrow*
おきます	おきよう	*wake up*
きます	きよう	*wear, put on*

D

ます form	Plain form	English
します	しよう	*do*
りょ行します	りょ行しよう	*travel*
うんてんします	うんてんしよう	*drive*
来ます	来よう	*come*

E

2 べんきょうしよう *Let's study from 1 p.m. till 5 p.m.* **3** 来よう *Let's come here again next week.*
4 かって　みよう *Let's buy and try this wine.* **5** あげよう *Let's give Robert a present.* **6** 出かけよう *Let's go out together tomorrow.*

F

1 りょ行しよう **2** やめ, てつだおう **3** そうじした, せんたくした, しよう **4** はたらき, 行こう
5 ねる, 書こう **6** 見た, 食べよう

G

1 やめよう **2** りょ行しよう **3** わすれよう **4** 書こう

H

1 いっか月ぐらい　ひとりで　ヨーロッパを　りょ行しようと　おもって　います。
2 まだ　ヨーロッパを　りょ行した　ことが　ありませんから。
3 むすめさんと　いっしょに　ピアノを　ひきたいですから。
4 ふじ山に　のぼろうと　おもって　います。
5 たばこを　やめた　ほうが　いいと　おもって　います。

I

2 (7) **3** (2) **4** (5) **5** (1) **6** (4) **7** (8) **8** (6)

J

Example: 私は　来年、いっか月ぐらい　日本へ　行こうと　おもっています。とうきょうへ　行ったり、
ふじ山に　のぼったり　する　つもりです。きょうとや　大さかや　ならへも　行こうと　おもって
います。できれば、ひろしまと　ながさきへも　行きたいです。・・・

K

1 三年間, 語 **2** 一, 好 **3** 学校, 四月 **4** 木, 男, 二人

Unit 17

A

ます form	Plain negative present	Plain negative past	English
かいます	かわない	かわなかった	buy
つかいます	つかわない	つかわなかった	use
あいます	あわない	あわなかった	meet
まちます	またない	またなかった	wait
もちます	もたない	もたなかった	hold, carry
入ります	入らない	入らなかった	enter
のります	のらない	のらなかった	get on
飲みます	飲まない	飲まなかった	drink
休みます	休まない	休まなかった	rest
えらびます	えらばない	えらばなかった	choose, select
あそびます	あそばない	あそばなかった	play
あるきます	あるかない	あるかなかった	walk
行きます	行かない	行かなかった	go
およぎます	およがない	およがなかった	swim
いそぎます	いそがない	いそがなかった	hurry
なくします	なくさない	なくさなかった	lose
話します	話さない	話さなかった	talk
あります	ない	なかった	exist, have

B

2 もらわなかった 3 行かない 4 およがなかった 5 ない 6 分からない 7 すわない

C

ます form	Plain negative present	Plain negative past	English
ねます	ねない	ねなかった	sleep
食べます	食べない	食べなかった	eat
わすれます	わすれない	わすれなかった	forget
とめます	とめない	とめなかった	park, stop
出かけます	出かけない	出かけなかった	go out

入れます	入れない	入れなかった	*put in*
かけます	かけない	かけなかった	*put on (glasses)*
います	いない	いなかった	*exist*
見ます	見ない	見なかった	*look, watch*
かります	かりない	かりなかった	*borrow*
できます	できない	できなかった	*be able to, can*

D

ます form	Plain negative present	Plain negative past	English
します	しない	しなかった	*do*
べんきょうします	べんきょうしない	べんきょうしなかった	*study*
しんぱいします	しんぱいしない	しんぱいしなかった	*worry*
ゆっくりします	ゆっくりしない	ゆっくりしなかった	*relax*
来ます	来ない	来なかった	*come*

E

1 来なかった 2 食べなかった 3 見なかった 4 いない 5 できない 6 うんてんしない

F

2 としょかんで 話さないで ください。 3 パスポートを なくさないで ください。
4 やくそくを わすれないで ください。 5 ここに 車を とめないで ください。
6 ここで しゃしんを とらないで ください。 7 ここで たばこを すわないで ください。
8 しんぱいしないで ください。

G

1 入れない 2 食べない 3 もたない 4 いそがない 5 かけない 6 飲まない

H

1 しない 2 ねない 3 かえらない 4 あそばない 5 のらない

I

い adjectives

Affirmative present	Negative present	Affirmative past	Negative past
<ruby>大<rt>おお</rt></ruby>きい	<ruby>大<rt>おお</rt></ruby>きくない	<ruby>大<rt>おお</rt></ruby>きかった	<ruby>大<rt>おお</rt></ruby>きくなかった
<ruby>高<rt>たか</rt></ruby>い	<ruby>高<rt>たか</rt></ruby>くない	<ruby>高<rt>たか</rt></ruby>かった	<ruby>高<rt>たか</rt></ruby>くなかった
いい	よくない	よかった	よくなかった
あつい	あつくない	あつかった	あつくなかった

な adjectives

Affirmative present	Negative present	Affirmative past	Negative past
しずかだ	しずかじゃ　ない	しずかだった	しずかじゃ　なかった
きれいだ	きれいじゃ　ない	きれいだった	きれいじゃ　なかった

Nouns

Affirmative present	Negative present	Affirmative past	Negative past
<ruby>学生<rt>がくせい</rt></ruby>だ	<ruby>学生<rt>がくせい</rt></ruby>じゃ　ない	<ruby>学生<rt>がくせい</rt></ruby>だった	<ruby>学生<rt>がくせい</rt></ruby>じゃ　なかった
<ruby>雨<rt>あめ</rt></ruby>だ	<ruby>雨<rt>あめ</rt></ruby>じゃ　ない	<ruby>雨<rt>あめ</rt></ruby>だった	<ruby>雨<rt>あめ</rt></ruby>じゃ　なかった

J

1 <ruby>時間<rt>じかん</rt></ruby>が　ありませんでしたから。

2 メイルを　<ruby>読<rt>よ</rt></ruby>んだり、<ruby>電話<rt>でんわ</rt></ruby>を　かけたり　しました。

3 3<ruby>時<rt>じ</rt></ruby>に　ひるごはんを　<ruby>食<rt>た</rt></ruby>べました。

4 さいふを　わすれて　しまいましたから。

5 とても　<ruby>長<rt>なが</rt></ruby>くて、おもしろくなかったです。

6 ロバートさんと　たなかさんと　<ruby>飲<rt>の</rt></ruby>みに　<ruby>行<rt>い</rt></ruby>って、10<ruby>時<rt>じ</rt></ruby>ごろまで　カラオケを　しました。

7 <ruby>何<rt>なに</rt></ruby>も　しないで、うちで　ゆっくりしようと　おもって　います。

K

Example: けさ、<ruby>時間<rt>じかん</rt></ruby>が　なかったから、あさごはんを　<ruby>食<rt>た</rt></ruby>べないで　かいしゃへ　<ruby>行<rt>い</rt></ruby>った。3<ruby>時<rt>じ</rt></ruby>まで
ひるごはんを　<ruby>食<rt>た</rt></ruby>べなかった。7<ruby>時<rt>じ</rt></ruby>まで　メイルを　<ruby>読<rt>よ</rt></ruby>んだり、メイルを　<ruby>書<rt>か</rt></ruby>いたり、<ruby>電話<rt>でんわ</rt></ruby>を
かけたりした。しごとが　おわった　<ruby>後<rt>あと</rt></ruby>で、<ruby>友<rt>とも</rt></ruby>だちと　えいがを　<ruby>見<rt>み</rt></ruby>に　<ruby>行<rt>い</rt></ruby>ったが、<ruby>長<rt>なが</rt></ruby>くて

つまらなかった。それから、レストランへ　ばんごはんを　食^たべに　行^いった。ばんごはんは
おいしくなかった。あしたは　しごとの　後^{あと}で　飲^のみに　行^いかないで　ジムへ　およぎに　行^いこう。

L

1 五月五日, 子　**2** 毎日, 六時　**3** 七本　**4** 日本, 八月

Unit 18

A

1 やくそくした, 来る　**2** 読^よむ^く, できる　**3** おしえた, 分^わかる　**4** おくった(おくる), つく　**5** しって いる
6 食^たべない

B

1 さむ, なる　**2** はれる　**3** ある, 来^こない　**4** やすく, かう, できる　**5** 飲^のまない　**6** ねて　いる

C

1 いたい, 休^{やす}む　**2** ふる　**3** つまらない, やめる　**4** しゅっせきする, できない　**5** 間^まに　あわない　**6** ある, 来^くる

D

1 食^たべる　**2** たりない　**3** かう　**4** はたらかない　**5** のぼった, ある　**6** しんぱいして　いる

E

3 今年^{ことし}の　なつ休^{やす}みに　ヨーロッパを　りょ行^{こう}する　ことに　しました。
4 毎日^{まいにち}　やさいを　食^たべる　ことに　して　います。　**5** 来月^{らいげつ}　国^{くに}へ　かえる　ことに　しました。
6 いつも　バスに　のらないで、あるく　ことに　して　います。　**7** べつべつに　はらう　ことに
しましょう。

F

2 おしえる, なりました　**3** 入^{はい}る, あらう, なって　います　**4** たつ, なって　います　**5** すむ, なりました
6 うんてんする, なって　います

G

1 今月^{こんげつ}　かいしゃを　やめて、来月^{らいげつ}から　大^{おお}さかで　はたらく　ことに　なりました。
2 今月^{こんげつ}の　22日^{にち}に　ひっこしします。
3 ロバートさんと　たなかさんが　てつだって　くれます
4 一^{いっ}しゅう間^{かん}ぐらい　りょ行^{こう}しようと　おもって　います。
5 エドワードさんの　そうべつかいが　あります。

H

2 この メイルは ロバートさんが 書きました。3 この しゃしんは エドワードさんが とりました。 4 この しごとは 私が やります。5 この えは すずきさんが かきました。

I

Example: けいこさん、おげんきですか。私は 今の かいしゃを やめて、きょうとで はたらく ことに なりました。あたらしい しごとが はじまる 前に、すこし 時間が ありますから、りょ行したり、ふじ山に のぼったり しようと おもって います。 ふじ山の ちかくに 友だちの やまかわさんが すんで いますから、あう ことが できるかも しれません。けいこさんは 今しゅうの 日よう日 ひまですか。 友だちが 私の そうべつかいを ひらいて くれます。できれば 来て ください。

J

1 毎日, 二十本 2 二千二十二年 3 本, 九百円 4 十二月二十五日 5 三百六十五日

Unit 19

A

1 行かなければ 2 飲まなければ 3 書かなければ 4 話さなければ 5 見せなければ 6 ぬがなければ

B

2 しゅっせきしなくても 3 いそがなくても 4 行かなくても 5 つくらなくても 6 はらわなくても 7 来なくても

C

1 飲まない 2 うんてんしない 3 休んだ 4 やめた 5 かけない 6 れんらくした 7 見ない

D

1 かいものして いる 2 読んで いる 3 して いる 4 行って いる 5 話して いる

E

1 ねて　いる **2** 見て　いる **3** べんきょうして　いる **4** いる **5** 入って　いる

F

1 ふらない **2** わすれない **3** 来ない **4** はじまらない **5** さめない

G

1 は, が **2** は, を, が **3** は, が **4** と, で, を **5** は, が **6** に, が **7** の, に, に, を **8** が, を, は, と, を

9 へ, を, に

H

1 あしたから　二日間、しごとで　大さかへ　行く　ことに　なりました。

2 午前　5時はんに　おきなければ　なりません。

3 午前　7時の　しんかんせんに　のる　よていですから。

4 かいぎに　しゅっせきしなければ　なりません。

5 ロバートさんは　かいぎで　あたらしい　コンピューターソフトの　はっぴょうを　します。日本語で　はっぴょうを　しなければ　なりませんから、ロバートさんは　きんちょうして　います。

6 大さかじょうへ　行こうと　おもって　います。

7 午前　9時から　11時まで　また　かいぎが　ありますが、午後は　何も　しなくても　いいですから。

I

Example: あした、しごとで　きょうとへ　行く　ことに　なりました。午前　6時はんの　しんかんせんに　のりますから、午前　5時に　おきなければ　なりません。それから、たなかさんに　あって、1時間ぐらい　話さなければ　なりません。午後　2時から　かいぎに　しゅっせきしなければ　なりません。日本語で　あたらしい　せいひんの　はっぴょうを　しなければ　なりません。かいぎは　4時に　おわります。かいぎの　後は　何も　しなくても　いいですから、アンさんと　きよみずでらへ　行こうと　おもっています。それから　8時の　しんかんせんで　とうきょうへ　かえります。

J

1 車, 百万円 **2** 毎, 時半 **3** 火曜日, 日本語, 行 **4** 毎週, 書

Unit 20

A

1 なかった **2** あった **3** ふった **4** もらった **5** のった **6** ひいた

B

1 かえった **2** 飲んだ **3** 出た **4** なった **5** おわった **6** ついた

C

1 ふって **2** 読んだ **3** かえって **4** けっこんした **5** ちょ金して **6** 行って **7** あった

D

1 わるかった **2** 高くて **3** つまらなかった **4** あつくて **5** いたくて **6** さむかった **7** りょ行したかった

E

1 おもしろくなくて **2** いそがしくなかった **3** ねむくて **4** よかった, 高くて **5** おいしくなくて **6** 行きたくて

F

1 ひまだった **2** かんたんで **3** きらいだった **4** 好きだった **5** 雨で **6** 学生だった **7** むりだった

G

1 たいへんで **2** 下手で, れんしゅうした **3** きらいで **4** きれいで, やすくなかった
5 ふべんで **6** いい　天気で **7** レストランで, おいしくなかった

H

1 一年ぐらい　イギリスで　えい語を　べんきょうしたいと　おもって　います。

2 べんきょうしながら　アルバイトを　しようと　おもって　います。

3 なつ休みに　アジアや　中国を　りょ行したいですから。

4 えい語の　きょうしに　なりたいと　おもって　います。

5 やさしくて　あたまが　いい　人と　けっこんしたいと　おもって　います。

6 小さい　いえを　かいたいと　おもって　います。

7 じぶんの　かいしゃを　つくりたいと　おもって　います。

I

Example: 私は　今、ぎん行いんです。しゅみは　りょ行を　する　ことです。しごとは　たのしいですが、いつも　とても　いそがしいです。ひまな　時間が　ありませんから、りょ行を　する　ことができません。三か月ぐらい　ヨーロッパを　りょ行したいですから、しごとを　やめる　ことにしました。イギリスと、フランスと、ドイツへ　行こうと　おもって　います。時間が　あったら、イタリアとスペインへも　行きたいです。日本へ　かえったら、じぶんの　かいしゃを　つくりたいです。

J

1 東南 2 来週, 東 3 一, 北海, 行 4 西口 5 人口, 六千四百万

GLOSSARY OF GRAMMATICAL TERMS

Conjugation	Conjugation refers to several forms words can take according to features such as tense, etc.
Particle	In Japanese, particles are added after nouns and sentences to indicate what roles they play in sentences, such as the subject, the object, etc.
Topic	The topic of a sentence is often marked with *as for* in English. Topics are followed by comments about them. For example, *As for John, he lives in London*.
Subject	*John* in the following sentence is the subject: *John ate ice cream*.
Object	*ice cream* in the following sentence is the object: *John ate ice cream*.
Volitional form	The volitional form is one of the several forms Japanese verbs can take. It expresses intentions to do something.

Short glossary of verbs, listed by unit: the Roman numerals I, II and III indicates the verb groups.

Unit 2

おきます II	wake up	たべます II	eat
ねます II	sleep	のみます I	drink
はたらきます I	work	みます II	see, watch
いきます I	go	ききます I	listen
きます III	come	よみます I	read
かえります I	return	かきます I	write
します III	do, play (sports)	べんきょうします III	study

Unit 3

あります I	exist (inanimate)	います II	exist (animate)

Unit 4

かいます I	buy	あげます II	give
あいます I	meet	もらいます I	receive
はなします I	talk	くれます II	give to me

Unit 5

おもいます I	think	

Unit 6

なります I	become	

Unit 7

わかります I	understand	あそびます I	play, enjoy oneself
あります I	have		

Unit 8

みせます II	show	つかいます I	use
でかけます II	go out	まちます I	wait
おしえます II	teach, tell	もちます I	hold, carry
でます II	exit, leave	しにます I	die
とめます II	stop, park (vehicles)	えらびます I	choose
つけます II	turn on	やすみます I	rest
つくります I	make	およぎます I	swim
はいります I	enter	いそぎます I	hurry
まがります I	turn	けします I	turn off

Unit 9

おきます I	put	すいます I	smoke (the cigarette)
たちます I	stand up	かります II	borrow
すわります I	sit down	かします I	lend
あけます II	open (the window)	うんてんします III	drive
しめます II	close (the window)	せつめいします III	explain
とります I	take (the picture)	けっこんします III	get married

Unit 10

ふります I	rain	しります I	know
かけます II	make (a phone call)	すみます I	live
ならいます I	learn	きます II	wear (clothes)
うります I	sell	れんらくします III	contact

Unit 11

つれて　いきます I	take (someone)	かんがえます II	think
おくります I	escort (someone)	わすれます II	forget
しょうかいします III	introduce	やります I	do
あんないします III	show around	まちがえます II	make a mistake

てつだいます I	help, lend a hand	なくします I	lose
はきます I	put on (shoes, trousers)	おとします I	drop, lose
かぶります I	put on (a hat)		

Unit 12

できます II	be able to, can	のぼります I	climb
ひきます I	play (stringed instruments)	はらいます I	pay
かきます I	draw (a picture)	りょこうします III	travel

Unit 13

おわります I	finish	ちょきんします III	save money
はじまります I	begin, start	ひっこしします III	move (house)
やめます II	quit, give up		

Unit 15

そうじします III	clean (a room)	いります I	need, require
せんたくします III	wash (clothes)	つかれます II	be tired

Unit 17

あるきます I	walk	かけます II	put on (glasses)
のります I	get on (transport)	しんぱいします III	worry
ぬれます II	be wet	ゆっくりします III	relax
いれます II	put in		

Unit 18

おくります I	send	しゅっせきします III	attend
つきます I	arrive	あらいます I	wash
たります II	be enough	ぬぎます I	take off (clothes)
はれます II	clear up	ひらきます I	give (a party)
まに　あいます I	be in time		

Unit 19

かいものします III	shop	かかります I	take
さめます II	get cold (temperature)	きんちょうします III	be nervous
ひきます I	catch (a cold)	とまります I	stay (overnight)

Unit 20

つづけます II	continue	そつぎょうします III	graduate
れんしゅうします III	practise		

(な) signifies it is **na**-adjective.

Unit 5

いい	good	いそがしい	busy
わるい	bad	たのしい	enjoyable
おおきい	big	ゆうめい(な)	famous
ちいさい	small	にぎやか(な)	lively
たかい	high, tall, expensive	きれい(な)	clean, beautiful
ひくい	low	しずか(な)	quiet
やすい	cheap	しんせつ(な)	kind
ながい	long	げんき(な)	healthy, cheerful
みじかい	short	ひま(な)	free (to have free time)
おいしい	delicious	べんり(な)	convenient
おもしろい	interesting, funny	すてき(な)	attractive, wonderful
むずかしい	difficult		

Unit 6

すばらしい	wonderful	すずしい	cool
つまらない	boring	さむい	cold
おおい	many	かんたん(な)	easy
すくない	few	たいへん(な)	hard, tough
あたたかい	warm	いや(な)	disagreeable, unpleasant
あつい	hot		

Unit 7

すき(な)	like, fond of	とくい(な)	good at
きらい(な)	dislike	にがて(な)	poor at
じょうず(な)	good at (skill)	ほしい	want
へた(な)	poor at (skill)	いたい	sore, painful

Unit 10

しんせん(な) fresh

Unit 11

しろい white

Unit 15

はやい quick わかい young

Unit 19

ねむい sleepy

Unit 20

ふべん(な) inconvenient むり(な) impossible

Japanese verbs usually have a very regular conjugation pattern, except for あります (*exist*), いきます (*go*), します (*do*) and きます (*come*). The first two verbs belong to Group I while the latter two belong to Group III.

ます form	て form	Plain form	Plain form past tense	Plain negative form
あります	あって	ある	あった	ない
いきます	いって	いく	いった	いかない
します	して	する	した	しない
きます	きて	くる	きた	こない